CW00641202

The Christian Com

The Christian Commitment

Essays in Pastoral Theology
(Mission and Grace, vol. 1)

Karl Rahner

Sheed and Ward
London

CONTENTS

THE CHRISTIAN COMMITMENT

1

THE PRESENT SITUATION OF CHRISTIANS: A THEOLOGICAL INTERPRETATION OF THE POSITION OF CHRISTIANS IN THE MODERN WORLD

There is a preliminary observation to be made before I embark on my real theme. I think that what I am going to say is, in itself, more or less right. But for this opinion, I would not be saying it. But this does not necessarily carry with it the conviction that this right thing that I want to say is the thing which here and now needs saying: that this right thing may not perhaps be out of place, so that it would be more right to say some other right thing. Suppose you say: "In twelve hours this house will be cut off by floods"; the information can scarcely fail to be of some interest to the inhabitants of the house. But it might, according to circumstances, be still more important to tell them that the roof is on fire and they had better get out.

It is not easy both to say the right thing and to say it in the right place. I am not, from this point of view, altogether sure that my remarks have the necessary qualification of urgency, and that they do not fail to say things which would be much more important at the present moment. So if, in the end, it seems to you that I have for the time being gone off in the wrong direction, though still remaining on the ground of truth, i.e. of what is right in itself, I shall be glad to hear from you about it. It can, of course, also happen that one judges more

immediate and urgent matters falsely through being unwilling
to listen to something fundamental but less immediate and
urgent.

The theme of this conference is: The theological interpretation of the position of Christians in the modern world.

The wording requires me to speak not as a politician or a
historian of ideas or a philosopher or a prophet, but as a theologian. A theologian speaks on the basis of Scripture and
Tradition as interpreted by the teaching Church. This gives
him a relatively easy basis for speaking of the position of the
Christian in the world. He can speak of the nature of man, of
his destiny, of nature and grace, of what is included in the
concept "the world," of the orders of creation and redemption,
of the meaning of history, of sin and redemption, of the working out of both of them on the secular plane of man's existence,
of the relationship between Church, people and State, of the
relative self-subsistence of the different areas of cultural life,
of the natural law, and of numerous similar things and norms
which are always to be found in God's world, which is also
the world of Christ and of the Church. But my task is *not* to
speak of these things. For I am to say something, as a theologian, about the *theological* interpretation of the position of
Christians in the *modern* world. Can anything be said of this,
theologically?

It is a world which did not exist when there came forth that
word of revelation which the Church preserves and proclaims
and with which the theologian is concerned. Of course there
still exists today the world of creation, sin, redemption, and
movement towards the future things of God of which revelation speaks. The world of Scripture is our world too. And if
we direct our gaze towards that in our world which revelation
explicitly sees in it, which revelation expresses of it, then we
are undoubtedly seeing what is most important in it, and something which always deserves and needs to be considered afresh.
But we should not then be seeing the modern world *as modern,*

i.e. that in it which makes our world different from any earlier one, that in it which has not always been the case, not even always and everywhere in the age, the *aion,* of Christ—precisely *our* situation, not that of any earlier generation of Christians. Can we, indeed, say anything theologically about *that?* We can of course, in regard to this present modality of the world, by which it is differentiated from preceding epochs, say all the things which Christians can always say: that it is something created and yet subject to evil, that it is subject to evil and yet redeemed and, in Christ, assumed by God into grace; that it is entrusted to human freedom and yet in the hand of God, that it has meaning and yet can only move onwards towards that fulfilled and real meaning which God will give in his future judgment. But to consider all this (and it would be an important consideration) would still be to fall back into that general kind of evaluation of which we have said already that it is not our present task.

Are we to say, then, that in so far as the special character of our age is not simply one more instance of the general Christian interpretation of the world, it can only be, for the Christian as such, a matter of indifference, and hence not a theme for theological consideration? But in that case the world, in itself, is a matter of indifference, undifferentiated matter, in which the Christian, as such, operates according to his otherworldly Christianity, until, like the characters in *Everyman,* he strips off what is no more than the costume of the part he has played and goes into eternal life taking with him only that part of him which he could just as well have enacted in any other role. In that case, the Universal is everything, and the Particular, the historically unique, is nothing, is non-being. In that case, we should have nothing to say of our particular theme except that we have to recognize that we are always dealing with the same world, with the Christian always in the same relationship to it. But if this is not so, if the present world as such, in its historical uniqueness, is a concern of Christians, how is the theologian to know anything about this present world, precisely in its modernity, *from revelation?* At the time when that historic word of revelation, to which nothing can be added, was uttered in Christ, this present world did not exist.

If we are to suppose that anything was said *then* about this world of *today,* it can only have been by way of prediction. But is there any such prediction? Does the message of Christianity include any such prophecy of our age, enabling us to say something theologically about our age as such? Or are we as Christians able only to declare what is always and universally valid, and then apply it to the case in hand?—in which process we shall always be dogged by the feeling that our principles are assuredly sound and good, but the attempt to apply them can be successful only to a limited extent, with the most important point of all left open: it could never yield any unambiguous conclusions because, having regard to this age as a whole, any such application of principles would rest upon an interpretation and analysis of our situation itself made not by theological but by purely personal means, thus always remaining our own, highly questionable work.

We are of the opinion that such a prediction does exist, and determines the Christian's position in our modern world. It is, obviously, not in the nature of an advance description of our time. This, for one thing, because divine prophecy is never a satisfaction of human curiosity about what is going to happen but a help in steering a Christian course through a future which is unknown and remains unknown; an illumination of the meaning of the future, but still leaving it dark, not history written in advance. Moreover, this applies particularly to our present case, since we could not expect that so small a section of time as concerns us here would be described in advance by the predictive word of God in such fashion that we could gather from it any kind of soothsaying prognosis of the future. But that little which the word of God gives us can nevertheless illuminate our present situation, even though it still leaves us in darkness and does not relieve us either of our cares or of responsibility in decision.

But before we can attempt to say what it is that God has predicted concerning our time, there are one or two premises to be laid down which, while they are theologically valid for all periods, appear to be particularly important in our own situation.

In the sphere of secular, worldly living, there is never any period that can be called *the* Christian age, any culture which is *the* Christian culture, etc. This does not only mean that according to Catholic teaching there are always Church and State, redemptive history and secular history, nature and grace, and that these can never be adequately united in one thing. It means rather that it is never possible simply to deduce, from Christian principles of belief and morality, any one single pattern of the world as it ought to be. In principle, there is neither in respect of the state, nor of economics nor of culture nor of history any one clear, concrete imperative which could be deduced from Christian teaching as the one and only possible right course. It is possible to reject certain conditions, tendencies, endeavors and actions as contradicting the Christian law of faith and morality. In numerous *individual cases* it may be that man's area of freedom in choice and action is in the concrete so narrow that there is in fact only *one* line of action remaining open to him as permissible or obligatory, if he wants to avoid offending against the Christian law; further, Christian principles, which give the structure of reality itself as offered to man's freedom to work on, may be of the greatest and most beneficial significance for human activity, and any violation of them may have the direst consequences. But it is never, in principle, possible to say in the name of these principles that the world is or has got to be precisely "thus and so," when "thus and so" means something ultimate, positive and individual. In principle, there can in one and the same situation be several possibilities of action, not only practical but also justified. The choice between these possibilities, which has to be made and always involves an historical human decision, cannot, in principle, be settled in advance in the name of Christianity. To deny this would be not only to refuse that right and proper dualism of which we have already spoken its reality or at least its right to reality; it would be, beyond this, an ontological heresy, since it would be an assertion that concrete events in the human sphere are *only* limiting instances of the universal, with no significance over and above that of the universal expressible in universal norms.

All this may seem a truism. But it is nevertheless extremely important in practical terms. It means, for instance, that nothing is ever *the* Christian culture, *the* Christian education, *the* Christian political system, *the* Christian party, etc. There can at most, in principle at any rate, be things which are unchristian in so far as they definitely contradict general Christian norms; there can be Christian cultures, systems of education, parties, etc., in so far as these are, in principle, in intention, and to some degree in practice, in harmony with these norms; but there can never (apart from the Church herself) be any single concrete thing in the sphere of world history and culture which can lay claim to be, in principle, uniquely and exclusively *the* Christian realization of anything. This implies that any earlier age which may have called itself Christian was not only often, in fact, very unchristian but was also, even taking the most favorable view, only *a* and not *the* expression of the Christian spirit. Hence no aspect of it is binding on us; not only because "times have changed," meaning the conditions surrounding human free action, but in any case, since it could, even at the time, have legitimately been otherwise. The fact that we do not always see this so easily, that, for instance, we speak with facile romanticism of the Christian Middle Ages and enthuse over "the West" in the name of Christianity (and not, as is permissible, in the name of our own historical, freely-chosen decision) is because the area of free choice *then*, the creative possibilities historically existing *then,* were relatively restricted, not because of Christian principles but because of geographical, technical, economic and other factors; so that *at that time* any general desire to exist in a Christian fashion probably was almost bound to produce what in fact was then produced. But this was, to repeat, something done because of historical necessity, not (as often supposed) because of the essence of Christianity.

From this it follows that as soon as there is any appreciable widening of the area of practical human possibilities, as soon as any considerable number of things, hitherto impossible, become possible to human freedom, the Christian in this historical situation at once discovers the sharply painful nature of choice. That is to say, it is only in these circumstances that a Christian comes explicitly to realize that he cannot use his Christian principles to supply a clear imperative for his activity at the historical level. They leave him in the air; meaning that they demand to be respected and put into practice in whatever course of action he may decide upon, but they cannot tell him what to decide; for, given the circumstances we have described, he is suddenly, as never before, presented with a multiplicity of legitimate possibilities, all of which could be ways of being a Christian.

No one would try to deny that this present age, the end-product of the modern period, does present us with this wide possibility of choice, carrying with it both the pain and the noble potentialities of freedom, or that it does so to an overwhelming degree. In the fields of technology, economics, sociology, mass psychology, etc., things are possible today which were impossible in earlier centuries. It is the simple truth that we are beginning to live in an age in which all that lies before it seems to shrink together into a single period.

From this two things, among others, immediately follow: (a) It will now become plain, in the clearest possible way, that Christians *as such* simply do not have any ready-made, concrete program for the conduct of the state, or of culture, or of economics, and in fact *cannot* have one. This was indeed theoretically the case in earlier ages as well. But it did not appear so plainly, because the area of possibilities historically available for human realization was relatively narrow. It is now going to become gradually clear that the gap between universal Christian principles and the putting of them into practice in any one of a number of possible forms is a gap as wide as the possibilities now opening up before us. From this it follows that we Christians should indeed rejoice that it is given to us to have the true standards by which human living can be shaped according to its meaning (their importance, and the importance of clearly recognizing them by the saving and searching light of revelation, has grown all the greater in face of the greater possibilities, now grown to monstrous proportions, of ignoring them to our own hurt); yet we cannot *as Christians* have any single, unitary program, when it comes to planning in the concrete. It may be that in some given, temporary situation we have to stand together because of a radical threat to Christian and human values. It may also be that in some given situation Christians, in their historical activity as *human beings,* in making their decision on some particular thing, without being required to do so precisely in the name of Christianity, happen to decide, more or less together, on one particular course. But they cannot bolster up either of these unities by saying that the norms of Christian conduct clearly lay down this one particular way, which is alone to be approved and chosen as providing the right course among the bewildering profusion of possibilities stretching around us.

What is immediately at work at the historical level is not the unchanging norms (though their effect, for good or ill, will indeed make itself felt at that level), but some one determinate, formative pattern and plan, as concrete as the actual activity which puts it into practice. This is what we Christians *as such* cannot have. We never have had one, for even in earlier times the particular concrete form given to the Christian ideal was not determined by Christianity as such (though indeed by Christians) but by other historical forces and influences. But it was possible in earlier times to *confuse* the original principles, and the practice of them, with a particular ideal at work at the historical level, and to regard this synthesis as final and obligatory. On this matter we of today are disillusioned, or we ought to be. We Christians have grown poorer. What we have lost is, of course, merely the illusion that because we were the people who listened with faith to the Word of God, we therefore had a complete recipe for the world's problems in our pockets, and the only difficulty was to be accurate and faithful in putting it into practice. It is useless to commend our Christian principles to the world as its salvation. What it wants is to hear concrete proposals. We have got to have the courage to act as human beings with a task in the world of history, and so to come forward with such proposals. But we cannot propagate them in the name of Christianity.

It is here that we find the really profound reason for the withdrawal of the Church from politics. Such a withdrawal involves neither opportunism nor a failure to proclaim and defend Christian principles. It arises from the realization that, in itself, fundamentally, if politics means having a concrete program, then there cannot be any one Christian form of politics, whether in the economic, constitutional, cultural or any other field. We must acknowledge this poverty in ourselves, if we want to be honest; and even here, honesty is the best policy. If we are honest about this "impoverishment" of Christianity, due to the clarification of the diastasis between Christianity as such and any particular concrete form given in the past to it, then Christianity will be divested, in men's minds, of that responsibility for particular historical states of affairs with which it is still involuntarily burdened today. If we are not honest about it, i.e. if we make some synthesis of Christian principles and our own historical preferences and then propagate that as what Christianity itself unconditionally demands, to stand or fall by it, then people will take us at our word in this false declaration. They will then, unavoidably, combat Christianity itself if ever they take some other historical decision than ours and set about implementing it, for it is we who have declared ours to be a pure and simple case of Christian principles in action.

There is this to consider, too. It is no doubt true that there do exist in this world forces of evil, of organized godlessness. There are not only differences of opinion and taste which can be settled by democratic compromise, being all equally justified in principle. There is, beyond these, a more and more concrete opposition between good and evil, and this does not mean a dialectical tension which ultimately makes harmonious sense because it keeps hauling the wagon train of world history in one constant direction. But true though this is, and real though its consequences may often be, we Christians cannot for all that be Manichees and believe in a real, absolute evil, still less in an incarnation of any such evil. In other words, we see as Christians that evil has power only through the good which is in it, and which derives from God. So if we refuse to see the programs and performances of anti-Christians, even the most extreme of them, simply as the embodiment of evil and nothing else; if we seek for the good in them, without which they would be powerless to achieve anything; if we refrain from committing ourselves, irrevocably and in advance, to the view that any such good is always adequately embodied already in our own admirable programs and mediocre performances (for we are in fact often sinful and short-sighted) —we are not then guilty of cowardly compromise or cloudy universal tolerance but are performing a Christian duty, since it would be heresy, not Christian firmness, to believe that there is an absolute evil as there is an absolute good.

The vast range of possibilities now opening out as a field of historical human decision calls for an active entity capable of availing itself of those possibilities; and the very width of the range confers upon any such entity an importance as new and as immeasurable as the new opportunities themselves, by comparison with earlier entities active in the historical process and with the possibilities open to them in earlier ages. This means that organized human society has taken on an importance, because of these new possibilities, which it has not had before. It is not for the Church to be that which actually and directly responds to such historical possibilities in the secular sphere. But something must be; such an entity is positively forced into existence (or into a new mode of existence) by the development of the possibilities themselves. It can only be the state or the community of peoples organized at a planetary level. Any other would simply not be capable of exploiting these possibilities. But this implies, whether we like it or not, that the state (either individual or planetary) is taking on an importance which it has never had before.

The opportunities for moulding human existence arbitrarily, according to plan and choice, used to represent a very small sector of human life in comparison with what was determined by natural conditions or done by smaller communities. The state, with its policies and its legislation, was able to bring relatively little to bear, in the way of conscious planning, on human life. Things have changed. Furthermore, the possibilities are such that the practical realization of them *cannot* be simply avoided. Hence they will in fact be realized. In other words, there will be a state (if indeed there is not already), whether regional or world-wide, in which the concentration of power will be gigantically vast in comparison with anything which has borne the name of state in the past. And this will happen even if Christian principles of subsidiarity and so on are respected. For the state has no need to take to itself anything which other, smaller corporations or individuals have *hitherto* disposed of, being capable of handling and controlling it themselves. It need only take to itself those possibilities, insistently clamoring to be used, which are entirely new developments, and which no one and nothing else would be capable of handling. These alone are enough to make it such as to inspire fear at first sight; to make it, indeed, a very disquietingly dangerous structure, as dangerous as the potentialities which the modern age places at its disposal. It is quite impossible that the state (whether regional or world-wide) should continue to be what we have been accustomed to in the past in such matters as: world population; the scope and needs of technology; problems of mass psychology in a vast and crowded population; ways of waging war; economic and cultural modifications in the way of life of individual peoples. Even with the most favorable possible outcome, i.e. maximum justice, the sphere of the state is going to outweigh that of private life; not because the sphere of private life has shrunk but because that of the state has expanded, the increased potentialities offered by the present historical situation being such that nothing else but the state could possibly handle them.

We have to take account of all this when we come to ask ourselves: What, as shown forth in the prophetic word of God, is the present position of the Christian, through which the situation as so far described acquires its special character?

My thesis is this: In so far as our outlook is really based on today and looking towards tomorrow, the present situation of Christians can be characterized as that of a diaspora; and this signifies, in terms of the history of salvation, a "must," from which we may and must draw conclusions about our behavior as Christians.

Before I try to explain and demonstrate the real heart of this thesis, there is one concept which I must explain as being extremely important to it. I have said that the diaspora situation is, in terms of the history of salvation, a "must." This needs explaining. There are, on the one hand, things which ought to be, *a priori,* unconditionally: such things, for instance, as are expressed in the ten commandments. There are, on the other hand, things which simply are, though they ought not to be; whether they are due to guilt or to misfortune one simply recognizes their existence, and that is all there is to it, except to bear them patiently if they cannot be changed and otherwise, at best, to try and eliminate them from the world. Between these two classes of things—things that ought to be, and things that ought not to be but simply are—there is a third, intermediate group of things and events and relationships. They ought not really to exist; that is to say, they are in contradiction with some rule of what should be, some ideal, some postulate; but they are not simply the factual contradiction of a rule. When they come into existence, and continue, they acquire, despite their conflict with what ought to be, a queer sort of justification and validity, a kind of inevitability, significance and value. It is impossible, and wrong, simply to endure them or simply to protest against them. Though they have not, properly speaking, any right to exist, yet one cannot simply eliminate them or struggle wildly against them. One ought rather to give them their due; to reckon with them; to draw certain conclusions from their existence (which, "considered in itself," they ought not to have, but which has, in the concrete, its own validity)—conclusions which will, in their turn, present us with an "ought," and this because these things, precisely *as existing* (and not simply as something to be grimly endured or fought against) have a significance for salvation.

I would like to say of such things, conditions and events that, in terms of the history of salvation, they are things which *must be,* basing myself in this on scriptural usage. For the Scripture witnesses to such things. When, for instance, our Lord says: "The poor you have always with you," this is something more than a statement about the persistence of a distressing fact. It does not dispute the necessity "in itself" of continually striving to the end that there shall be no poor, that they shall no longer exist. Still less is it a denial that the mode of poverty can change enormously within the changing modes of social relationships. Nevertheless, the existence of poverty is not ranged among those mere facts whose sheer existence can only be acknowledged under protest. Although, in the last analysis, there are poor people only because there is guilt, yet this fact is acknowledged as something that *must* be, something to be reckoned with, so that to exclude it from the maxims of practical activity would be to commit the fault and error of unchristian idealistic utopianism. Anything that is, in this sense, a δεῖ in terms of the history of salvation is often spoken of in Scripture as willed by God, as "having" to be, as signifying salvation, as calling for man's active acknowledgement, even though "in itself" it ought not to be at all.

The supreme instance of such a "must" in the history of salvation is the Cross of Christ, for it was necessary that the Son should suffer. He had to suffer, although it was by human guilt that he did suffer. He did not see his passion (although it was something that *ought* not to happen) as something which he should take all possible steps to avoid; he did not say to Peter, "Yes, you are right, it must not be, and we will do our utmost to avoid it, only unfortunately it will happen all the same." He said, "Go behind me, Satan . . . thou savorest not the things that are of God, but the things that are of men" (Mt. 16, 23). So too elsewhere: scandals and schisms "must" come; not merely they *are* coming, but they *must* come, for all that it is woe to them by whom they come. Hence we conclude that it is possible and permissible for a Christian to affirm a "must" of this sort within the history of salvation, to reckon with it as such, and to draw from it conclusions involving an "ought" for his own conduct, even though it does not itself arise from any *a priori* "ought," but from historical causes and even from human guilt and failure.

Fault and failure in our proper historical task need not always consist in refusing the right kind of combat (which is also our duty) against the facts of this world; it may consist in combating them with an unchristian utopian radicalism, refusing to acknowledge them for what they are. There is a wrong way of working to eliminate poverty; there is a wrong kind of obstinate, pseudo-heroic apostolate which refuses to shake the dust from its feet and go into another city when the message falls upon deaf ears. All the New Testament prophecies about the hard time that the Church was to have in history were made not only to prevent us from being too dismayed, but also so that this historical situation of the Church, not "as it ought to be" but nevertheless foreknown, should be something from which we can draw conclusions for our own conduct.

We cannot here go on to provide a more precise ontological and theological basis for this concept. Taking it for granted, we proceed to the next assertion: that our situation as a diaspora is for us today a "must" of this kind in the history of salvation. This means that we have not only to acknowledge this diaspora situation as unfortunately permitted by God but can recognize it as willed by God as a "must" (not as an "ought"), and go freely on to draw our conclusions from this.

But first we have to look at the fact itself. The mere fact of being a diaspora on this planet has had to be gradually admitted. Whether it is a happy choice of words, or theologically correct, to speak of the countries of Europe as mission countries can be left an open question. But that there are no longer any Christian countries (with the *possible* exception of the Iberian peninsula) is a fact. Christianity (though in very varying proportions) exists *everywhere* in the world, and everywhere as a diaspora. It is effectually, *in terms of numbers,* a minority *everywhere;* nowhere does it fill such a role of effective leadership as would permit it to set upon the age, with any force or clarity, the stamp of a Christian ideal. Indeed, we are undoubtedly in an era which is going to see an increase in this diaspora character, no matter what causes we may assign to it. The new age of Jesus Christ, as prophesied by Lombardi, is certainly not going to dawn for some considerable while. On the contrary, the Christendom of the Middle Ages and after, peasant and individualistic petty-bourgeois Christendom, is going to disappear with ever-increasing speed. For the causes which have brought about this process in the West are still at work and have not yet had their full effect.

But that we are a diaspora throughout the world is not merely a fact to be recognized *a posteriori* and with dismay. It is something which, on the basis of our faith, we should have expected, in the sense of a "must" within the history of salvation. It is foretold, though of course only as an implication which could be made explicit only by reference to certain facts in the present world situation. It is a theological datum which can be interpreted according to faith. It is something which "ought not to be," in so far as all men ought to become Christians when the message of faith is preached to them (which to a certain measure has been done all over the world), and in so far as the peoples of the West ought not to have fallen away from Christianity. To this extent, the Christian desire *not* to be a diaspora remains, of course, an obligation on every Christian, a desire which cannot fail to inspire apostolic activity and witness, both active and passive. But between this grimly heroic desire and the merely dismayed recognition that it has very small success there can and should lie something intermediate: the knowledge of this diaspora situation as a "must" in the history of salvation, and the valid conclusions drawn from this historical knowledge.

Every earthly institution wants to make good; it measures its internal self-justification in terms of its palpable, immediate chances of total victory. But to Christianity and the Church her Founder promised not only that she would endure until the end of time but, just as clearly, that his work would always be a sign of contradiction and persecution, of dire and (in secular terms) desperate combat; that love would grow cold; that he, in his disciples, would be persecuted in the name of God; that the struggle would narrow down to an ever more critical point; that the victory of Christianity would not be the fruit of immanent development and widening and a steady, progressive leavening of the world but would come as the act of God coming in judgment to gather up world history into its wholly unpredictable and unexpected end. This permanent state of contradiction, foretold to the Church and the Christian as a "must," is something that we must not water down. It does not simply mean that each generation has to be Christianized afresh, and that this always comes hard to every member of the human race. It is not only a matter of contradiction and friction in individual private existence, in which everyone, being a sinner, is capable of resisting the message of the Gospel. Scripture sees the contradiction as a fact of public life and universal history, a matter of peoples and politics. Hence this contradiction is a "must" in the history of salvation.

Why is the universal diaspora situation prophesied as a "must" in this sense? This needs explaining.

This is our starting-point: That the Church and Christianity will be to the end of time a stone of stumbling and a matter of contradiction; that this will not simply happen to be so as a matter of fact, but is a part of that mysterious "must" (appearing constantly in Scripture) in which human guilt, which ought not to exist, yet remains within God's plan; that God does not will man's guilt, and yet this guilt, which is not willed, is used even "in advance" as a means to the working-out of the divine plan.

For a believer, who judges things from God's standpoint, a "must" of this sort is not merely something with which he *may* reckon, but something with which he *must* reckon; something that he must calmly expect and at which he must not be surprised.

Given this contradiction of the Church—permanent, public, to be expected from the start and not to be wondered at—how is it going to manifest itself?

As long as the Church was in practice limited to one cultural and historical sphere (e.g. the West), the contradiction could come "from outside," simply because there *was* an "outside." Hence the Church and Christianity could, within that restricted area, be "omnipotent," the unquestioned, uncontradicted leader and ruler, and still have her opponents "from outside": heresies (ultimately of oriental origin) and Christendom's hereditary foe, the Turks.

From the very moment (a moment which may, of course, need centuries to develop its full potentialities) when there is no longer any such "outside," both because the Church has become actually world-wide and (the two interacting on each other) because the histories of separate peoples have merged into one single history of mankind, every people and every historical situation becoming from then on a force *within* every other one—from the very moment when this happens, the contradiction of the Church, in terms of theological history, can no longer come from "outside" and *must* (in that mysterious sense of must which is our present concern) arise within Christendom as such, in the form of schism and apostasy. For otherwise, either the Church would be uncontradicted or else she would still be to some extent an historically insular Church, belonging to one particular separate culture. Neither is possible.

In fact we see that the beginnings of schism and the dechristianization of the West through the Reformation and the Renaissance and Enlightenment do in fact appear at just that moment when, on a substratum of European expansion, the Church begins to be in actuality a world-wide Church. In the moment when she begins to be a Church of *all* the heathen, she also begins, everywhere, to be a Church *among the heathen*. The actual combination of these events is, of course, loaded with guilt and tragedy; but seeing it at the higher level of theology, and of a theology of history, it is nevertheless included within a mysterious "must"; something that should not

be a surprise or a scandal to a believing Christian, because it
was in fact to be expected, as indeed he has to expect the continuance of guilt and of rejection of Christ even to the end of
time. The loss of the Church's medieval omnipotence in public
life (it is best in this sense to reckon the Middle Ages as end-
ing with the French Revolution) was then, theologically,
something to be expected, however much it may have involved
guilt as well. The value given to the Church in the public life
of society, state and culture in the Middle Ages cannot be
regarded as something demanded by the very nature of the
Church; not if the Church is bound to be, permanently, the
Church of contradiction and if it was also to be, and had in
fact become, a world-wide Church. The medieval form was
possible only so long as the Church was the Church of a more
or less closed culture. It became impossible from the moment
when the West became an integral part of world history. From
then on the contradiction had to be either everywhere or nowhere. Since it cannot be nowhere—it has to *be*—it must be
everywhere. "O foolish and slow of heart . . . ought not Christ
to have suffered these things?" applies to his sufferings in world
history as well.

Furthermore, the value set upon the Church in public life, in
its medieval form, is not attributable, as a phenomenon, simply
and solely to the supernatural power of the Church and Christianity. That particular form (not the Church's essential theological value) was also, at least in its factual, existential
realization, the result of temporal, secular combinations of historical forces. It was a fact rather of cultural history than of
theology. One might say that every "Middle Ages" (i.e. every
culture resting on a peasant and small-city foundation, and
remaining historically stationary for a whole period) has its
ruling religion, established in unchallenged supremacy; this
without reference to whether such religion be true or false,
from below or from above, medieval Islam or medieval feudal
Shintoism in Japan or anything else. What reveals the super-

natural power of Christianity is not so much the mere fact that
it, like other cultural religions, did in one particular culture
and one particular, necessarily passing stage of that culture
exercise a practically unchallenged ruling power over the
hearts of men and their cultural institutions. This argument,
dear though it is to many apologists, will not seem entirely
convincing to an historian or a philosopher of history. It is
rather that, on the one hand, when this secular and temporary
historical situation disappears, Christianity then manifests,
even empirically, and despite all apostasies and other losses,
an incomparably greater power of resistance and endurance
than other religions which have also known their similarly
favorable "Middle Ages"; and, on the other hand, that the
Church's position in the Middle Ages can be seen as having had
a providential significance in enabling Christianity to make as
powerful an entrance as it did, both moving *out of* and moving
with that limited culture, into the world at large, and so become, empirically, a world religion.

Hence we have a full right, indeed almost a duty, to take account of the fact, without any sense of shock, that the form of
the Church's existence in public life is changing. The fact that
the Church is becoming a diaspora *everywhere,* that she is a
Church surrounded by non-Christians and hence living in a
culture, in a state, amidst political movements, economic activity, science and art which are conducted *not* simply and
solely by Christians—all this is a "must" in the history of salvation. From this "must" we are permitted and indeed en-
joined to draw sane and sober conclusions in the shape of
maxims to be applied to our pastoral work for the offensive
and defensive activities of the Church and of Christians. Such
conclusions bear a dialectical relationship to a maxim (which
is at the level of "ought") that we apply to the spread and
defense of Christianity, which demands that we try with all
available means to win all men and all aspects of culture for
Christ. Nothing less than the dialectical unity of both sets of

maxims can constitute the full law governing our position as Christians in the present age.

Before we go on to the implications for our attitude as Christians to be drawn from this diaspora situation as a prospective characteristic of the present age of the Church and a "must" in the history of salvation, we must give some consideration to the elements of the diaspora situation itself.

Let us simply ask ourselves: What happens, what is bound to happen, when a Christian has to live his Christianity among a large number of non-Christians? A great many things follow of themselves:

(a) His faith is constantly threatened from without. Christianity receives no support, or very little, from institutional morality, custom, civil law, tradition, public opinion, normal conformism, etc. Each individual has to achieve it afresh for himself; it is no longer simply "a heritage from our fathers." Each individual must be won to it afresh, and such a recruitment can appeal only to personal decision, to what is independent and individual in a man, not to that in him which makes him a homogeneous part of the masses, a product of his situation, of "public opinion" and of his background. Christianity ceases to be a religion of growth and becomes a religion of choice. Obviously Christians will still give institutional form to their lives, over and above the institutional element in the Church herself: they will try to transmit to their children the faith that they have themselves won in a personal decision, they will develop and try to preserve Christian habits of morality, customs, practices, associations and organizations. But by and large the situation will remain one of choice, not of natural growth, of a personal achievement constantly renewed amid perilous surroundings.

(b) A considerable part of the riches of culture—literary, artistic, scientific—upon which a Christian too lives and *must* live, unless he wants to become a hopeless outsider in the intellectual life of this world, will not be specifically Christian, nor bear the stamp of Christianity. Much of what is institutional in social, civic, political and cultural life will be such as to exercise a negative influence on a Christian's moral life, and will bring his life into almost unavoidable conflict with his Christian morality. The non-Christian world, which (though we love to assert such things of it) is *not* a sheer mass of decomposition and deterioration, will even seek to develop its own forces, its own institutions of a social, intellectual, educational and moral kind, and these will certainly not be so obliging as to prove a mere series of desperate and unsuccessful efforts. These things will then make an impression on Christians, and refute our cheaply repetitious (and theologically false) propaganda to the effect that anywhere where the Church and the clergy are not in control and do not supply the principles of action, there can be nothing but disintegration and decay.

(c) The Church of the diaspora, if it is to remain alive at all, will be a Church of active members, a Church of the laity: a laity conscious of itself as bearing the Church in itself, as constituting her, and not being simply an object for her— i.e. the clergy—to look after. Wherever this new kind of Church exists or comes to be, the laity will have to be given this possibility in fact, and not only on paper; the laity will have ecclesiastical duties which they, as a matter of course, carry out, and rights, as they did in the early Church; they will not be simply people to whom such-and-such orders are given in such-and-such a case, and who are expected to count it an honor to be allowed to do something for the hierarchical Church, meaning the clergy. *Sociologically* speaking, the Church of the diaspora has the character of a sect, in contrast to that of a Church of the vast mass of people, a Church *in possession,* and hence, sociologically, confronting the individual not as something constituted and sustained by himself but as independent of him and over against him; the diaspora Church has the advantages that her "sect" character gives her, and the duty constantly to overcome the dangers inherent in it. The Church of the diaspora rests permanently on the good will of her ordinary members. The Church of the diaspora will be the Church of an age in which other institutions, state and cultural, will be exercising functions in the field of education, research, creative culture, etc., which were formerly exercised by the Church; for the diaspora Church will be, to a large extent, quite unable to exercise such functions any longer, since these functions address themselves to the *whole* population, and for this reason, and others too, cannot devolve upon what is only a *part* of civil society. It follows that the Church of the diaspora will be more immediately religious in aspect. This is not because this Church of the future will not have her principles, applicable to every cultural field, which she will seek to realize through the Christians working in those fields; it is because as a sect (sociologically speaking) she cannot directly set the tone in the realm of culture in the way that she could when the vast mass of people belonged to her. Hence in what she directly does she will of her own accord concentrate on what is her own most vital sphere, even if no one confines her by force to the church and sacristy or drives her into the catacombs.

(d) The clergy will no longer belong automatically to the upper, privileged levels of society. To be a member of the clergy will not, in the long run, continue to be, to the extent and in the sense that it has been hitherto, a "status" in the sociological sense. It remains a status in the Church, but it will not always be, to the extent that it has been, a status in secular society.

(e) In general, we shall not have so much of *the* Church and *the* State confronting each other, whether in conflict or concordat. For this relationship of the past was based upon the fact that everyone (or nearly everyone) was simultaneously both a citizen and a member of the Church. In the future, contacts between Church and State will tend to take place within the individual and his conscience. For the State is no longer so much the Government or a monarch, but rather the, precisely, *non*-Christian (for the most part) population (no matter what the constitution may be: the patriarchal State is in any case a thing of the past). And this population is, for the most part, uninterested in the particular Christian interests of one part of it; nor is the Church any longer an organization whose direct political power could be of any great significance.

It would be possible to enumerate many more things of a similar sort which can be seen to follow, given a little psychology and sociology, from the fact of a religious communion living, growing and preserving itself in an indifferent or hostile environment: a Church of the diaspora, now and for the foreseeable future. It seems to me that much depends on our fully and freely recognizing this fact and courageously accepting its conseqences. Such an outcome is not so much a matter of course as might be supposed. We have still not fully wakened from our dream of a homogeneous Christian West. It often leads us to react furiously and in a false context when something happens to shake us out of the dream; we often seek, again in a false context and with inappropriate means, to realize this dream-ideal, and so apply ourselves to the wrong point altogether. I had better refrain from giving examples. For it would inevitably be possible to discuss each of them *in utramque partem,* since any particular effort aimed at a *limited* objective and intended as a *partial* realization of a homogeneous Christian West could well be *both,* as such, misconceived *and* nevertheless, in the circumstances, correctly regarded as justified and necessary on other grounds. I can only ask you to think over what I have said (supposing it to be new to you, which I expect it is not) and then, as occasion arises, to test by it the manifestations of Catholic life which you encounter: Must they, ought they to be, what they are, if we are to regard the diaspora situation not only as a sheer disaster (calling for one legitimate response and one only, that of grim resistance) but also as a preordained "must" (not "ought"!) in the history of salvation?

If we now go on to ask what follows from this situation, we are going beyond the theme as originally set, since it referred to the situation, not to its consequences. But since the rest of this conference has been concerned with other problems, we have sufficient grounds for thus overstepping the bounds of our theme. So:

(a) We must first stress once more that our diaspora situation is not just a fact but a "must" in the history of salvation. This means that we cannot simply approve of it as something justified in advance. Our relationship to it is not that of the ancient Jewish people to the Gentiles, who were from the start, i.e. by the will of God in advance of any guilt, left out of the covenant. We cannot cease to be missionary; we have to want the number of Christians to increase, to want their influence, their importance, the concrete realization of a Christian spirit in public affairs and social institutions, to grow; we have to try to diminish the contrary of these things. But despite all this, our growing diaspora situation is something to be expected, something foretold, something we can count on and which need not cause us any inner conflict or missionary defeatism. It is foolishness, not high principle, to suppose that because something was brought about by guilt in the first place, its effects must necessarily be removable: to think that there is a permanent and universal duty to aim deliberately and directly at eliminating something by, so to speak, fanatically intolerant frontal attack, merely because its coming into existence involved guilt. This is wrong in the sphere of individual life, and equally wrong in the wider sphere of history. Though we must keep our missionary fervor, there is nevertheless a right sense in which we must adjust ourselves to the diaspora situation and come to terms with it. Not only interiorly, with faith and serene trust in God's direction of all things, and reverence for his will, positive and permissive, by which good is brought out of evil. It has to be in our outward behavior as well.

The objection might be made that if as Christians we are supposed to remain missionary, and even on the offensive, what is all this about coming to terms with the diaspora situation as a "must" in the history of salvation? Isn't this demanding coexistence and co-validity for principles of Christian behavior in public life which are in fact incompatible? No, the principle of coming to terms with the fact of the diaspora does not contradict the duty to maintain a positive missionary spirit, and it does have a practical bearing on outward behavior. It makes us realize that there can be points over which we do *not* need to take the offensive, where we can let things take their course and come to terms with them, precisely so as to work away with all our available and limited resources, interior and exterior, at other points where it makes sense to do so, and thus not waste our energies in the wrong place. Throughout her history the Church has constantly come to terms with unavoidable situations, once they were established, without thereby betraying God or herself. But how many times she has tried to go on too long fighting the inevitable, and so wasted her energies in the wrong place when they were wanted elsewhere. The theoretical realization that the diaspora situation is a "must" in the history of salvation should be a help in guarding against this danger.

What, after all, does a person do if he sees the diaspora situation coming and thinks of it as something which simply and absolutely must not be? He makes himself a closed circle, an artificial situation inside which it looks as if the inward and outward diaspora isn't one: he makes a *ghetto*. This, I think, is the *theological* starting-point for an approach to the ghetto idea. The old Jewish ghetto was the natural expression of an idea, such that orthodox Judaism was ultimately bound to produce it from within itself: the idea, namely, of being the one and only chosen people, wholly autonomous, as of right, in every respect, including secular matters, and of all other nations as not only not belonging in practice to this earthly, social community of the elect and saved but as not in any sense called to it, not an object towards which there is a missionary duty.

But a Christian cannot regard his Church as autonomous in secular, cultural and social matters: his Church is not a theocracy in worldly affairs; nor can he look upon non-Christians as not called; nor can he with inopportune or inordinate means aim to get rid of the "must" with which the history of salvation presents him, namely that there are now non-Christians in amongst the Christians or real Christians in amongst the non-Christians. His life has to be open towards the non-Christians. If he incapsulates himself in a ghetto, whether in order to defend himself, or to leave the world to the judgment of wrath as the fate which it deserves, or with the feeling that it has nothing of any value or importance to offer him anyway, he is falling back into the Old Testament. But this is our temptation, this ghetto idea. For a certain type of deeply convinced, rather tense, militant Catholic at a fair (petty-bourgeois) cultural level, the idea of entrenching oneself in a ghetto is rather alluring; it is even religiously alluring: it looks like seeking only the Kingdom of God. Here we are, all together, and we can behave as though there were nothing in the world but Christians. The ghetto policy consists in thinking of the Church not only as the autonomous community of salvation (which she is) but as an autonomous society in every field. So a Christian has to consider Linden-Weber a greater poet than Goethe,[1] and have no opinion of any magazine except *Feuerreiter*[2] (I imply, of course, no criticism of this magazine nor of those who promote it); any statesman who makes his Easter duties is a great statesman, any other is automatically a bit suspect; Christian Democratic parties are always right, Socialists always wrong, and what a pity we haven't got a Catholic party.

The insistence, for the sake of the ghetto, on integrating everything into an ecclesiastical framework naturally means that the clergy have to be in control of everything. This results in anti-clerical feeling, which is not always an effect of malice and hatred for God. The interior structure of the ghetto conforms, inevitably, to the style of that period which it is, in make-believe, preserving; its human types are those sociological, intellectual and cultural types which belong to that period and feel comfortable in the ghetto: in our case, the petty bourgeois in contrast to the worker of today or the man of tomorrow's atomic age. It is no wonder, then, if people outside identify Christianity with the ghetto, and have no desire to get inside it; it is the sheer grace of God if anyone ever manages to recognize the Church as the house of God, all cluttered up as she is with pseudo-Gothic décor and other kinds of reactionary petty-bourgeois stuff. We may be preserved from this danger, which has become a reality only too often during the last few centuries, by a clear-sighted and courageous recognition of the fact that the diaspora situation is a "must" in the history of salvation, with which it is right to come to terms in many aspects of our practical conduct.

(b) If I now try, as I must, to give a few practical applications of this principle, by way of illustration, these are simply in the nature of samples, and the samples are not in themselves of great importance. If, for instance, we, in our mid-European, German-speaking world, clamor for a Catholic university, complete with all faculties, on the lines of the Italian universities, then we are asking, *rebus sic stantibus,* for a ghetto-university, and refusing to realize that we do and must live in a diaspora. If, again, we cry out for the Government to make laws to check the decline in moral standards, we are forgetting that we live in a diaspora and that all that this will do, in the long run, is to generate anti-clerical feeling in people who don't want to be burdened with enforced regulations laid on them by us. (I hope I do not need to stress that there are, of course, laws in this respect that are justified; but they have to be well-motivated, well-proportioned, and introduced with tact and intelligence.) Again, we shall simply have to accept, in many respects, the feelings that people have about life, of a cultural or uncultural nature. If people who like to go and roar in chorus at football games on Sunday (I don't happen to be one of them) are considered by us to be pretty well lost souls already, then our pastoral attitude is at least as distorted as their mentality is, perhaps, infantile and superficial. If people today regard the evening as the time for cultural activities, then we must have evening Masses; and attempts to convince them of the superior excellence of getting up early in the morning had better be left unmade. If people of today are, in moral matters, influenced by their environment, because they live in the diaspora and must live in it and, without thereby putting themselves in the wrong, *want* to live in it, then the Christian education and formation of their moral conscience—which is, inevitably, somewhat coarsened by their environment—has to start from some point where there is still an understanding tending towards a higher level, not at points where any such understanding is—unfortunately —simply not available, nor merely with the Church's formal authority in moral matters.

If our presentation of Christian principles is to be effective, then what applies to the winning of an individual must also apply to our public presentation of ideas amongst the masses: we must begin with things for which we can expect some understanding, and go on slowly step by step. A man's ability genuinely and existentially to grasp particular values (which is a necessary condition for *subjectively* grave sin) is very largely the product of his environment. We cannot countenance any departure from the objective moral norm. But our proclamation of Christian principles ought not to ignore the fact that there are not only in individual cases *causae excusantes a peccato formali* but, among Catholics living in the diaspora, general sociological causes: a hardness of heart which is socially conditioned and generally present. Have we asked ourselves searchingly enough what follows from this? —not, indeed, as regards moral norms, but as regards our practical pastoral attitude to people who were or are Christians according to their baptismal certificates but perhaps, because of the diaspora situation, have never been so in practice, interiorly, even if they do, for social reasons, pay their tax to the Church and send their children for religious instruction.

What, for instance, am I to do with a Catholic whose second "marriage" (invalid because of the divorce of one party) has been of moral benefit to him, because he does not see this second marriage as immoral, on account of his socially, culturally, historically conditioned hardness of heart (cf. the Old Testament situation), and its consequences for him, morally as well as in other ways, have been entirely happy? We are not going to assume, *a priori,* that in questions of this sort all further thought on more practically useful methods of applying general principles is bound to be entirely superfluous.

If we live in the diaspora, then—just another example— it is as important to teach young people how to read non-Christian books, periodicals and magazines, which they are going to read anyway, as to instruct them to take the Catholic papers. If we live in the diaspora, we cannot allow ourselves to produce, educationally, and to hail as the best, the type of layman who has the mentality of a *bien pensant* of the year something-or-other. If we live in the diaspora, then the office-job type of pastor will have to die out. For the only service available from the bureaucrat mentality, which does still exist, is one that has no real care for the public: a service of an institution, not of people. Have we the courage to break away from bureaucracy, office hours, routine, impersonal, non-functional organizational clutter and clerical machinery —and just do pastoral work? If a man can find in us another man, a real Christian, with a heart, someone who cares about

him and is really delivering the message of God's mercy
towards us sinners, then more is happening than if we can
hear the impressive and unmistakable hum of bureaucratic
machinery. Let us get away from the tyranny of statistics. For
the next hundred years they are always going to be against
us, if we ever let them speak out of turn. *One* real conversion
in a great city is something more splendid than the spectacle
of a whole remote village going to the sacraments. The one
is an essentially religious event, a thing of grace; the other
is to a large extent a sociological phenomenon, even though
it may be a means of God's grace.

When today all of us, clergy and laity together, in our different ways, do our pastoral work in the diaspora, we find
ourselves, *mutatis mutandis,* facing the same problem as in
the foreign missions. We may, in *our* mission, be guilty of
the same sorry fault as is represented there by Europeanism.
When we are trying to convert people to Christ, we want to
convert them to the cultural style which we have inherited;
which is perhaps something that belongs to us, but not to
them. Think of the appearance of the inside of many religious
houses; of the level of many of the products of "folk" religion;
of the unctuous tones of our religious talk; the narrowness of
our bourgeois horizons; our censorious attitude to a thousand
and one things in everyday life (hair styles and lipstick, for a
start)—and you will understand what I mean by this equivalent in the home missions to Europeanism in the foreign
missions. We cannot afford this kind of thing in the diaspora
situation.

If we are living in the diaspora, when we say or write anything in Church matters we must do so in the recollection
that non-Christians can hear and read as well as ourselves.
It is not all right to write, as did one prominent Catholic
newspaper, just *one day* after the announcement that the Pope
intended to define the new dogma, that the whole Catholic
world had rejoiced at the news; it is not all right to say (as

the same paper did) that the Pope was throwing open access to God's grace and mercy when he granted an indulgence to travelers by sea; it is not all right to put up notices on church doors in the Holy Year saying that to gain the latest indulgence the minimum requirement is to be in a state of grace, as though it were not particularly requisite in other circumstances.

If we live in the diaspora, it is not all right for the Catholic press, out of pure devotion, to give the impression that there is no public opinion in the Church, or ought to be none; that every criticism of anything the hierarchy does, however correctly expressed, is necessarily uncatholic; that it is, *a priori,* quite impossible that the hierarchy's actions should arise from human motives, mistaken information or a failure to recognize the needs of the day. It *is* uncatholic to be always assuming, on a basis of general anti-hierarchy feeling, that such things are so (and this does happen); but it is, equally, theologically false to assume that such things simply cannot be so. Something that A. Koch once wrote applies here: the time is past when it was possible to hope that real wrongs could be systematically hushed up and concealed, because suppressed truths turn poisonous and, living in the diaspora, we cannot afford to have a loyal opposition inside the Church perverted into a crypto-heretical underground movement.

(c) When we say that we have the right to make a cool, dispassionate reckoning with the fact that the Church is a diaspora, we mean, understanding it rightly, the very opposite of resignation and defeatism. If we once have the courage to give up our defense of the old façades which have nothing, or very little, behind them; if we cease to maintain, in public, the pretense of a universal Christendom; if we stop straining every nerve to get *everybody* baptized, to get *everybody* married in church and onto our registers (even when success means only, at bottom, a victory for tradition, custom and ancestry, not for true faith and interior conviction); if, by letting all this go, we

visibly relieve Christianity of the burdensome impression that
it accepts responsibility for everything that goes on under this
Christian top-dressing, the impression that Christianity is
natura sua a sort of Everyman's Religious Varnish, a folk religion (at the same level as folk costumes)—*then* we could be
free for real missionary adventure and apostolic self-confidence.
Then we should not need to sigh and say, "We *still* have fifteen
percent"; we could say, "We're up to seventeen percent already." Just where is it written that *we* must have the whole
hundred percent? God must have all. We hope that he takes
pity on all and will have all indeed. But we cannot say that he
is doing so only if we, meaning the Church, have everybody.
Why should we not today alter to our use, quite humbly and
dispassionately, a saying of St. Augustine's: Many whom God
has, the Church does not have; and many whom the Church
has, God does not have? Why, in our defeatism, which springs
from a muddled feeling of pity for mankind, do we forget that
it is not the truth but a heresy that there is no grace outside the
Church? If we would only rid ourselves of these prejudices,
grafted into us by the external Christianity of the West, we
should not then feel inclined to engage in combat only if we
immediately win a hundred-percent victory; we should then be
justifiably proud and thankful if we won just *one* new Christian,
instead of burying our ostrich heads in the shifting sands of
those who are Christians already.

In short, if we demanded less of ourselves, but that less the
right thing, i.e. not universal Christianity when the diaspora is
an inescapable "must," but a battle for new individuals, then,
though immediate statistics would not look any better, the real
state of our mission, in respect of its chances for the future,
would surely be improved. Then we would realize in practice,
not only in theory, that even in the diaspora the initiative can
really be ours. We feel on the defensive if we get the idea
(which is unfair to ourselves) that it is the Church's fault, because of her failures here and now (never mind what may be

true of the Church in the past), that there are so few Christians about. We are taking the offensive if we tranquilly accept the fact of the fewness of Christians *as a fact* and set about winning new ones. We cannot simply say in despair that we are losing more than we are gaining. It all depends on what we are losing and what we are gaining. One soul apostolically won from a milieu which has already reverted to paganism is worth more than three hung onto from the remnants of traditional Christianity (one would almost like to say, folk-costume Christianity), only to be, themselves or their children, lost after all; because, not having passed through the crisis of this age in its acuteness, they are not immunized against its spirit and so will not, perhaps, stand fast in the long run. What matters in these little local offensives is not so much the statistical, demonstrable successes they may show. The courage for an approach of this kind, and just one or two new Christians to show for it, already amount to a lot, sometimes to everything. Beginnings may be disappointingly meager; but they may amount to a victory here and now with unforeseeable consequences. St. Benedict did not know that he was fathering a new western civilization when he went out with a few monks to refound monasticism on Monte Cassino.

An apostolate on the offensive, not exhausting itself in desperate efforts to save what is beyond salvage (the Church considered *as identical* with everybody in a given area), need have no fear of being fruitless in the long run. The apparent atrophy of the religious sense today is a passing phenomenon; in the period of vast upheaval in which we live, of which the past century of industrialism is only the beginning, it was, *in concreto,* absolutely unavoidable and to be expected. Anti-clericalism, whether tacit, automatic and non-violent or—as it sometimes is, even today, partly through our own fault—actively provoked, will collapse, by and large, when it becomes clear everywhere that the Church desires only faith in God and love for him, and these only as the unforced decision of the human heart, not to be induced by any other means. Man's religious sense is ineradicable, nor can it, in the long run, be appeased by pseudo-objects provided by secular utopianism, economic, social or cultural. Even at the level of this world, Christianity's chances are greater than ever. And if this be doubted—I mean, the possibility of discerning such chances— well, it is precisely for the Christian to hope against all hope, knowing that God triumphs when we seem to be lost.

Of course, for all this we need faith in eternal life; a faith so strong that it is ready to purchase eternal life by the witness of earthly death. We are often lacking in this uncompromising faith. We have nothing, of course, against the possibility that after a tolerably pleasant life in this world there may be another, guaranteed better still. But the idea of directing one's life here according to this faith, in such fashion that anyone who does not share it is bound to think one mad—that's not for us. So we try by every means and with dubious zeal to demonstrate that Christianity is also the best and most reliable recipe for a happy life in this world, forgetting that the only way in which this can be so is precisely by not caring whether it is so or not. Even this hyperthrophied care for the things of this world arises from the ghetto mentality, the refusal to admit that we are living in the diaspora: we want to find some aspect of Christianity which will make it presentable anywhere. And the consequence of this is that there are Catholics who are Catholics by culture, by politics, by civic morals, but are not and do not want to be Catholics by faith. But in the diaspora situation, only he can endure to the end who truly believes in eternal life and in the promises of God.

NOTES

1. Or, as it might be, Francis Thompson or G. K. Chesterton a greater poet than Milton.
2. Or *Jubilee,* or whatever it might be.

2

THE ORDER OF REDEMPTION
WITHIN THE ORDER OF CREATION

The theme of the redemptive order seen within the order of creation is certainly one well suited to a diocesan Lay Apostolate conference. The apostolate of the laity operates chiefly in that dimension to which we apply the theological (and by no means easily intelligible) expression of "the world," and hence the "order of creation." But it is to be a Christian apostolate in this world; which means that it is to give their full scope to the forces of redemption, to shape the world in so Christian a fashion that in and through this activity the individual Christian can work out his own supernatural and eternal salvation. But this raises the whole question of the precise relationship between redemption and the world, grace and nature, heaven and earth: the question of what exactly it means to say that the order of redemption signifies a healing, sanctifying and glorifying of the world and, on the other hand, that God's grace is something essentially other than the natural created world. The theme surely states, too, the theological basis of the apostolic and missionary vocation of the layman, whose setting is not only the Church and the Church's life in the narrower sense, but the sphere of secular, civic, political, cultural, in short "profane" living.

As our development of the theme will show, the main thesis can be quite simply stated if, instead of placing the orders of redemption and creation alongside each other, we speak of the order of redemption *within* the order of creation; this states the thesis that divine grace, the fruit of the redemption, actually penetrates the created order itself, healing and sanctifying it; that it incorporates the world, in all its abiding naturality, into the *mysterium Christi;* and that this process of taking the world by grace into the life of God is also meant, according to God's will, to be carried out by the activity of men, and hence by what we call lay apostolic action.

The theme itself dictates how the discussion is to be divided. There must be a first section which aims at clarifying the unity, rightly understood, of redemption and creation. It must show that we can, and in what sense we can, and must, speak of a real unity of the two, though they are self-evidently not one and the same. There must then be a second section in which certain consequences are drawn from the matters considered in the first part; that is to say, it must be shown, in the concrete, how Christian existence consists in a life derived from this unity and directed towards its actualization.

1. The Unity of the Orders of Redemption and Creation

The first part of our discussion, then, concerns the order of redemption within the order of creation, i.e. the fact and nature of their unity. The first section of this first part will have to make a few clarifications and distinctions, simply for the sake of a more precise understanding of the most important concepts always encountered in an inquiry of this kind. The second section will then deal with the actual problem of the theme itself. A certain amount of overlapping between the sections is of course inevitable.

1. If we survey the terms used in scientific theology and in the everyday language of religious discourse, we notice that they include a whole series of mutually contrasted concepts. We speak of grace and nature, of the supernatural and natural

orders, of the law of the Gospel and the natural moral law, of
Christianity and the world, of the redemptive and created orders, of the Church and the world, of nature and supernature,
of sacred and profane, etc. The existence of distinctions of this
dualistic kind is not a matter for doubt. But even before we
come to the actual question of the precise relationship of these
constantly contrasted concepts to each other, and of their possible unity with each other, it is highly dangerous to regard
these pairs of concepts as all equivalent to each other. It gives
birth to lasting misunderstandings and to theses which are off-
balance if not just plain false. We must, at the risk of pedantry,
make this a little more precise at the purely conceptual level.
If, for instance, we are talking about nature and grace, the line
between the two runs quite differently from that which is involved when we are talking about the orders of creation and
redemption. If we talk about the Church and the world, we
are making a different distinction from that by which we distinguish between Christian life and the world.

Grace is something really distinct from nature, given, without obligation, by God to nature, which confers, primarily
upon man and through him in a secondary sense upon the
world, a participation in the divine nature and divine life.
Grace and nature stand thus over against each other as, in a
true sense, adequately distinguishable entities. This does not of
course impose, in advance, any conclusion about their mutual
relationship and unity. For if we consider the nature of grace
more closely, we must realize that it is essentially a determination, elevation and divinization of nature; that there is no grace
except that granted to a particular, concrete, natural created
reality as determining it; that it presupposes quite definite conditions in that nature as such or creates them for itself as pre-
requisites. Real grace exists only in *man graced*, in nature
graced as a divinization of precisely *that* nature. It is not a
sort of second story carefully placed on top of lower nature by
the heavenly Architect, in such a way that the ground floor is

kept as far as possible intact and just as it is in itself, serving in fact merely as a sort of base for the upper story; so that you can live in either of them without its mattering to whichever is, for the time being, the other one. There cannot be any grace which does not imply a quite definite putting into action of nature; nor can there be any human, responsible putting of nature into action which is not subject to the demands of grace, amounting *in concreto,* with no avoidance of it while life lasts, to a Yes or No to grace. But it is still true that grace and nature are two adequately distinguishable entities.

As soon as we start talking about the *order* of redemption and grace, we have something different. For if "the order of redemption and grace" is an expression covering everything which appertains to the concrete existence and practical putting into action of "grace" as the actualization of "redemption," then the term "order of redemption" includes the order of creation as an essential factor within it. The two orders are then still, indeed, not identical, but neither are they adequately distinguishable from each other; they are related as the whole to the part, as the whole consisting of presupposer and presupposed is related to the presupposition. Hence the two pairs of concepts *grace-nature* and *order of redemption–order of creation* cannot simply be taken as equivalent. The same would of course hold if instead of *order of redemption–order of creation* we said *supernatural order–natural order*. The supernatural order is that order established by the gracious will of God in which God's creation exists as a necessary factor and presupposition, so that the supernatural order is related to the natural as whole to part.

If we speak in modern terminology of the Church, we mean the community of the faithful organized socially and juridically by Christ, under the hierarchical direction of the Pope, and the bishops in union with him, in a common outward profession of faith, in a common cult, and in the life of the faithful as hierarchically directed in other respects. Without prejudice to the basic necessity of the Church for salvation, the Church as actually existing, understood in this full sense, is identical neither with the influence and effect of God's grace nor with the total life of the Christians who are her members. For according to Catholic teaching there is grace, and justifying grace, outside the Church too, true though it is that this grace does, in an effective sense, originate within the Church and "orders" a man to the true Church whether he realizes it or not. There are without doubt people who are justified in the grace of God but not in the strict and complete sense members of the Church, as this word must be understood and employed today according to official usage. The Church is not, then, coterminous with humanity as embraced by God's grace; the area of the Church and the area of effective salvation do not, at this moment in the history of salvation, simply coincide.

Nor can the lives of Christians who are actually members of the Church be described simply as "ecclesial" in the strict sense of the word only when they are acts of the Church as such: the preaching of the word of God, the active administration and passive reception of the sacraments, the other acts done in the Church on the basis of the *potestas ordinis* and the *potestas jurisdictionis*. Further, such acts of the laity as are done on the basis of an actual commissioning by the hierarchy, and so as an actual participation in the Church's hierarchical apostolate, are acts and events of the Church. But the patience of a mother, the bedside prayer of a child for his parents, the social understanding applied by an industrialist to his business, the decision of a statesman in the political life in which he participates in the spirit of the Gospel, etc., can and should be acts which are utterly supernatural, sustained by the grace of God, inspired by the spirit of the Gospel and by Christian moral teaching, and relevant to salvation; but they are not acts of the Church. They live by the life of the Church, but they are not the life of the Church herself. They are Christian, but not ecclesial.

The area of the Church and her action is not, then, coterminous with the area of supernatural, grace-bearing action on the part of her members. There is an area which forms part of the Christian's task, of his vocation and his responsibile action, which does indeed, in conformity with the nature of the Church, respond to the stimulus of the norms she proclaims and live by the power of God's grace in Christ, but which nevertheless cannot be directly determined and organized by the Church in her official, concrete existence. Hence it does not become an act of the Church herself, and is not "ecclesial" in that strict sense which would make it possible, *ratione peccati,* to claim all the moral activity of Christians and of men generally as falling within the Church's competence, or to attribute to the Church, to this extent, a *potestas indirecta* over everything that the faithful do. The field of the Church's activity does not simply coincide with that of Christian activity, for the *potestas indirecta ratione peccati* does not in fact mean that the Church is always in principle capable of taking the general moral precepts which she maintains and deducing from them a concrete imperative for concrete action on the part of her members in each individual case, and so of laying a concrete command upon them. This is exactly what is not the case, and hence the Church and her activity do not coincide with the Christian activity of her members, i.e. with Christianity in its concrete realization. Much of the action of Catholic Christians is both Christian and ecclesial, but much of the action of Christians who belong to the Church is action of Christians but not action of the Church.

Hence if we set the concepts of "Church" and "world" over against each other, we may be contrasting the Church with the unbelieving, godless world, self-locked against the offer of God's grace; but the same pair of opposites may equally well stand for the distinction we have just been analyzing between the Church's life and the Christian, supernatural life of Christians, which cannot be, directly, an object for concrete com-

mands from the Church as a hierarchical society. In making
this distinction we are not of course denying that it is precisely in this secular and Christian life of the Church's Christians, which is not the life of the Church, that the Church's
vital power and her salvational import for the world can and
must be manifested.

These considerations and distinctions, made here purely at
the conceptual level, show how necessary it is to be careful
about terminology. We cannot treat all the terms appearing
down one side of our series of pairs as interchangeable, if we
want to speak with any accuracy. We must have a care about
this if we do not want to involve ourselves in difficulties arising
not from the matter in hand but from bad terminology. Thus,
arguments about the lay apostolate have probably arisen to no
small extent from the failure to distinguish between an ecclesial
and a Christian apostolate of the laity; between an apostolate
directly commissioned by the hierarchy as a share in the hierarchical apostolate, and an apostolate in that field where the
Church neither has nor claims any direct, concrete power of
guiding and commanding, but where, nevertheless, truly supernatural, Christian acts are required for the salvation of the
Christian who does them and of the world itself.

2. With these preliminaries stated, we come now to the
matter in hand, though the first section has inevitably antici-
pated some of what now has to be said. Our subject is the fact
and the more precise nature of the unity of the orders of redemption and creation.

(a) First let us make some formal ontological observations
on the unity of a complex entity. Difficult though it may be for
formal ontology and logic to deal with, the created intellect is
faced with the fact that there are entities which are really *one*
and yet, within this unity and without ceasing to have it, do
include factors really distinct from each other. Unless we think
of this unity in a merely superficial way, on the imaginative
pattern of different things placed side by side and spatially

continuous, we have a real logical and ontological problem: The different factors really are different within the "one thing," and not deducible from each other; to pose one of them is not simply and self-evidently to pose another, or they would have to be simply identical; and yet these different factors must form a real unity, and hence there must be within this one thing a single principle constituting an ultimate unity, which both maintains the separateness of the many in the one and really and truly unites them in the primal unity. We have got to be able to understand the different individual factors, in their difference and their relative opposition, by means of one unitary principle of plurality.

These ontological relations vary essentially, of course, according to what particular plural unit is involved. The "one thing" which consists of quantitative parts; the one human being consisting of body and soul; the one spirit with its plurality of powers, etc., are all very different cases, in which this ontological mystery of a plural unity recurs analogically in very different ways. Let us merely indicate at this point, abstractly and formally, one case of an ontological unity-plurality dialectic, because this is the quickest way of obtaining a particular conceptual tool which we need here. I mean that plural unity in which something, in order to be able to be itself, calls into being something else, distinct from and presupposed to itself, sets it up over against itself and maintains it in unity with itself as a differentiated thing.

This is very abstract, but such a situation does plainly exist, and can surely be traced, as an ontological relation, at very various levels of being. To take just one example: Concrete bodiliness is certainly distinct from the spiritual. But it is not, in the concrete, simply something added, complete in itself, to the spiritual being, so that the question would then arise of how these two entities could be united as from outside them both. Anyone who has really understood the Church's teaching on the soul as the actualizing formal principle of the body knows what we mean when we say that the soul itself creates this bodiliness, which is other than itself, as something distinct from and yet united with itself, in order to achieve its own being, its own essential fulfilment as spirit; when we say that bodiliness is not accidental, but an essential presupposition which the soul creates for itself, distinct from itself, and thus, from its very origins, maintains in unity with itself. The usefulness of this concept to our present discussion will soon become evident.

(b) No direct assault on the question of the unity of the orders of redemption and creation can avoid (if we want to reach an intelligible solution) recoiling, however carefully, on theses which are a matter of theological dispute. If we state our questions with that degree of precision which alone can produce answers, equally precise, with a concrete relevance to our lives, it is unlikely that they can be given any solution within the limits of pure dogma. One might no doubt try to limit oneself to what is unambiguously and dogmatically defined in the Church's teaching, so as to remain on the safest possible ground. But the moment one wants to clarify the scope and meaning of these dogmatically certain propositions, with reference to the concrete problems of life, it becomes impossible to avoid, altogether, the application of certain particular *theologoumena*. It makes no difference whether one notices this or not. Dogma concretely applied is inevitably dogma subjectively understood by a particular contingent and historically conditioned subject. But we shall nevertheless do our best to avoid such *theologoumena* so far as possible, and hence shall not need perhaps to speak explicitly about them and the theological disputes connected with them.

There is no doubt that creation, including man and his history, material and spiritual together, is, as originally conceived by God, a unity such that each thing in it is relevant to all the rest, and all the rest to each thing. This mutual interdependence, which is the ground of the unity of creation, is of course of the most various kinds, since within the unity of creation there exist the most various entities which, being essentially different from each other, cannot have simply the same functions in relation to each other. But we must say radically, and from the start, that Christianity knows nothing of *creations,* only of one *creation,* since the entities which God has created do not merely connect with each other in so far as they all go back to one and the same origin, but are also in communion with each other, and this applies to all of them.

The world of angels, for instance, ontologically remote from us though it seems, is nevertheless, as the world of "principalities and powers," related to the world of men and indeed to the material world; it belongs in the same history of salvation and damnation as the world of men, and within that history there is real interdependence. In relation to the material world, even an angel is not, in the Christian view, a Leibnizian monad. As for man, the truth that in him material and spiritual are combined in a true, substantial and, in terms of the doctrine of the resurrection of the flesh, final unity is, quite simply, a dogma of faith. In stating this dogma we are in fact stating that man cannot fulfil his spiritual nor indeed his supernatural life without embodying this fulfilment in material reality: without a turning towards the world, an infusing of the spiritual into the material. Hence the world is really a unity, one thing. The actual interdependence between everything and everything else corresponds to the original creative will of God, and takes shape in the essential mutual relationships, at the level of their very nature, which hold between individual things.

But within this one world there exists not only mutual relationship but also order, i.e. an objective gradation of degrees of being, of the worth and the effective power of each individual being within this one world. This order too is willed by God, or it would not exist. Now we have to say, on the one hand, that the totality of this one creation is willed by God as a totality, and hence that each individual (as is shown by the way its very nature is directed towards others) is willed by God only in so far as it is also a factor (though perhaps an absolutely irreplaceable and unique factor) in and for the one world: it is possible to say of every single thing, in a true sense, "This would not be if that were not also willed, and everything, great and lofty though it may be, exists for the sake of the rest." But because this single totality is willed as an ordered thing, the relation between the gradations of being, worth and significance can also be expressed by saying that everything lower exists for the sake of the higher, and so that everything in creation exists for the sake of the highest thing in this world. For we must always bear in mind that the creative action of God, which is in its divine origin absolutely and identically *one,* wills that the world should have, in the concrete, precisely this order of subordination and superiority, and the structure (if we may call it so) of the divine action can be read from the structure of what that action produces. We can then confidently say that God wills the whole of creation for the sake of the highest being in creation; and this proposition is not simply an application of the one we stated first, which is also true, namely that in this one world, in order that it shall be one, each thing must necessarily exist for all else, and all else for each thing; our second proposition expresses the equally important truth, as an effect of the action of God, that this one world is hierarchically ordered.

If we apply these formal considerations to the world in the concrete, we then have to say: within God's creation there is not only existence constituted as created by God out of nothing, infinitely different from and other than God; within this world there takes place the miracle of divine love, the self-communication of God to what he has created, when God himself, coming forth from himself in person, takes a created reality to himself as his own in the hypostatic union, and so truly empties himself and becomes a creature. If by creation we understand everything which exists externally to the inner divine life, then God's self-expression in that which is other than God (the incarnation of the Word of God) is the highest of God's creative acts. It is of this, then, that we must say that everything else in this one and hierarchically ordered world exists for its sake. We do not need to embark on the question of whether God would have become man if there had been no sin. This world, in the concrete, which God has willed, and has willed as one thing (without our needing to imagine, anthropomorphically, a series of divine decrees all, from God's side, depending on each other)—this world is a world in which God has allowed sin to exist and hence one in which the incarnation of the Word of God necessarily took place because of sin and for our salvation. But it is also a world in which this incarnation is the highest of the acts of God, to which all other entities essentially refer, and for whose sake everything else, including nature, the secular sphere and sheer matter, is willed by God.

Hence we can also say that the order of creation, even considered *as natural,* belongs to the order of redemption seen as the self-communication of God in that act in which the Word of God became a creature; that it belongs to it as a presupposition, distinct from redemption, which redemption itself creates for itself in order to be able to be itself; that therefore redemption graces the order of creation—precisely *this* creation—with itself, laying creation open to itself in all its dimensions and potentialities and giving to everything in it an ultimately supernatural meaning, but at the same time confirming it in its true and permanent naturalness and seeking to heal it wherever it is damaged.

(c) We need to say something further about this inner openness of the natural creation towards the divine self-communication in grace. It is not only that we can speak of such an openness in every natural creature towards grace, towards divine self-communication, towards a sharing in divine life, in so far as the whole of creation manifests, in the nature of angels and of men, a *potentia obedientialis* for grace; meaning that, if God wills, it can be the subject of a supernatural conferring of grace. We can speak of it, beyond this, in the sense that in the concrete order of supernatural divine self-communication as in fact willed by God, every natural created entity is ordered to this grace in such a way that it cannot remain really whole and healthy in itself, nor achieve the completion required by its own nature, except as integrated into the supernatural order of grace. In the concrete order, then, nature itself can find its way to its own completion only if it realizes that it is actually a factor within the all-embracing reality of grace and redemption. The "relative autonomy" of the natural physical and cultural spheres never extends, in Catholic teaching, to the implication that they can achieve even the significance which is their own and immanent to them, except through the grace of God in Jesus Christ. To miss supernatural salvation means missing natural salvation as well. Anyone who wants to persevere in keeping the natural moral law in its entirety needs the grace of Christ, even though this may need, in the first instance, to be only "entitatively natural."

This, in the light of what has been said already, precisely does not mean an alienation of the natural from the law of its own immanent being, nor an authorization to Christians to bypass this law immanent in nature for the sake of any directly supernatural and religious aim. We have said that it is precisely the natural in its natural structure that is presupposed and affirmed, in its natural validity, by the redemptive order as the very condition of the latter. The validity of natural structures of a secular, pre-religious, pre-moral and extra-ecclesial kind is precisely a requirement of redemption, which must be taken into account; it must be respected for the sake of the redemptive order itself. But precisely because, and in so far as, the natural order is the presupposed condition for the very possibility of the supernatural order, set apart from itself by the supernatural order itself, natural existence has, within the concrete order of total creation, an inner openness to grace and a real crying need for grace. But it follows from this that everything natural, if fully and freely experienced, accepted and realized as what it really is (i.e. necessarily supernatural in its ultimate goal) is actually always, at every stage, more than purely natural. For if one tries to achieve the "purely natural" in this concrete order, simply in its "purity," what results is not the purely natural but the guilt-laden merely natural, closed, to its own undoing, against grace.

What is a quite different question, of course, is whether and how far and in what way this quality in natural things of having a supernatural end needs to be consciously appreciated by the human beings who are experiencing natural things and giving them their realization. In a case, for instance, where the natural moral law is *de facto* being observed, the healing grace of God is *de facto* being given even if the person concerned does not know it and has not expressly desired it. But we Christians, at least, ought to be aware of this openness within all natural things directing them towards the ordering of grace. We ought not merely to be stating it as a theoretical fact, here and there, once in a way; we ought to be experiencing it more and more, in the concrete, in everyday life, and putting it into detailed practice. We need to be gradually waking up to the fact that the detailed events and actions of concrete human existence are always in fact, even in their very naturalness, something more than merely natural.

When, for example, a concrete human being (and whether he is aware of it or not is, in the first instance, immaterial) experiences genuine, personal love for another human being, it always has a validity, an eternal significance and an inexpressible depth which it would not have but that such a love is so constituted as to be a way of actualizing the love of God as a human activity springing from God's own act. Death, however much just a "natural death," when suffered by man is always *in concreto* a death which happens only because of the death

of Adam the sinner and of Christ on the cross. The only reason
why we take man so absolutely seriously, the only reason why
we *can,* and the reason why (whether we like it or not) we
must, is that God, in the Word who became man, has taken
man so absolutely seriously that it is only possible to take God
seriously if we take him seriously as man, and man, with a
divine seriousness, in him. All human realities have in fact,
even as natural, an unexpressed, perhaps merely potential, but
nevertheless truly Christian quality, and we can indeed address
to all earthly existence the words of St. Paul to the Athenians
(Acts 17, 23): "What you worship [we might say: actualize]
I preach to you"—namely, the God in whom everything exists
and lives and who is the God of redemption precisely as being
the God of creation, and *vice versa.*

God has not created two realities needing subsequently to
be, so to speak, harmonized. Rather, he has constituted the
whole of reality distinct from himself, to which he communicates himself, according to one ultimate, primordial intention,
so that it all has a primordial unity and every difference in it
springs from that unity as a mode of the unity itself, the unity
preceding the differences which arise from it and which must
precisely for its sake be respected. So if we want to formulate
the relation of the supernatural to the natural order, we can
equally well speak of the redemptive order within the created
order or of the created order within the redemptive order. I
mean that we can use each of these two concepts either as a
term for the totality of God's world as concretely existing or as
standing for one distinct factor within that whole order; and
according to which way we mean it, we can either say: The
redemptive order must develop within the created order as its
all-informing, healing, elevating and divinizing principle, even
though it is (as grace) more than the mere affirmation of the
world and its immanent natural structures; or else we can
formulate it as: The created order remains included within the
redemptive order (using this for the totality of the divine

order), in so far as it is a distinct, necessary factor within the redemptive order, having its own task in it and attaining to a share in the salvation of the whole order of things.

(d) We have so far been discussing this unity in diversity between the created and redemptive orders rather in terms of a theological and almost static ontology; there remains something essential to be said of it in so far as it is the determination of an historical world, and thus itself historically conditioned and determined. This unity is, in the true sense, real and permanently valid once and for all in that it is the object of God's unconditioned and all-powerful creative will, so that there could not be any world from which this unity could be simply eliminated; in particular, this unity is ultimately grounded in God's absolute decision, which no free creature has the power to alter, to express himself in his own Word's becoming a creature. But this unity is willed as the determination of a created order which God has willed as an historical unfolding; an order which is required to seek and attain the fulfilment of its permanent essential nature in the course of history. And to this extent the unity of the world of nature and of grace, permanent and indestructible as it is, also has its history. It is a unity which is to be realized; its achievement is a task entrusted to man. Speaking theologically, we can say that this unity, which is thus something to be historically fulfilled, is already eschatologically complete, and yet is to be realized through human beings; it is still unfinished, vulnerable and hidden. Of this there is more to be said.

Underlying this process, by which the unity is given its determination by the unfolding of the history of salvation, there is the fact that the relationship between the different factors in this one world is not simply a static relationship; the different elements, notwithstanding their permanent unity and their permanent differentiation, do in a certain measure approach or recede from each other, and their "*perichoresis*" (if one may so term it) can vary in degree and hence can have

a history. Indeed, we experience this directly in the fulfilment
of our own being: a man is one thing, in all his component
parts and dimensions; nevertheless he has to set about discovering this unity between the diverse capabilities of his mind,
his body, his soul, between personal choice and instinct, between interior and exterior, between integration within himself and openness towards the world, even though all these
factors are mutually conditioning each other right from the
start, and none of them can exist without the others. So it is
with the unity between the orders of creation and redemption.
They are one by the primeval creative will of God, and yet they
have to seek and find each other in order to become one. The
history of salvation and damnation is, at the same time, the
history of this unity as something to be achieved and whose
achievement is in danger.

The history of this unity has now entered upon its final,
eschatological stage, because the incarnation of the Word has
already happened and is no longer only something hidden
within God's decree; God has now definitively taken the world
as a whole, with all its indestructible ontological unity, into
his own life, by taking one of the factors in it and making it
personally his own, a factor which we call the humanity of
Christ and which, precisely in this divine assumption of it,
remains a factor belonging to the one total order of creation.
Since the incarnation of the Word of God as an act of the
divine compassion, it is not possible for there to be an absolute
split between the orders of creation and redemption, nor for
their union to be so rejected by man that it would remain only
in the form of the damnation and ruin of the created order. The
unity of grace and nature, working itself out as the blessed
salvation of nature and not its damnation, is already fundamentally and irreversibly achieved. In the incarnation and the
Cross God has made a total and final decision (without prejudice to human freedom) in favor of the world and the natural
order as saved, glorified and to be given beatitude through

the victory of grace. The drama is no longer in the balance; world history is already, in principle, decided, and the decision is for its salvation.

But given that this unity of the created and redemptive orders has already entered upon the eschatological stage (a unity both reconciled and reconciling), it is then inadmissible for a Christian, faced with the task of believing in this fact (improbable as it is, and seemingly contradicted at every turn by secular experience), to conduct his life, in the concrete, as though this unity were still historically in the balance. *Post Christum natum* he simply must be more optimistic in his thinking about the world than he need have been (or could have been) before he knew that the Word of God had taken to himself for ever the flesh of this world. He can be less suspicious, more trusting, in his approach to the world than his own experience alone would warrant. He actually must, out of faith in the incarnation, cherish an optimism about the world which could not but seem infantile and silly if his chances were to be judged simply in the light of worldly experience. Not that such optimism is entitled to forget that it is founded upon the Cross, the death, and so in secular terms the defeat, of the Son as far as the destiny of this world goes; nor that it is to be confused with secular utopianism, as is spasmodically done both by those with an unbelieving idealistic faith in progress and those with the Communist aim of making an earthly paradise by brute force. But it is when a man is free from such illusions, when, in disillusionment, he faces reality as it is, when he is aware of and suffers from dead-ends and defeat and death as the tragedy of everything in the world and of all culture, all engaged in reducing itself *ad absurdum*—it is precisely then that he is subject to the most hideous of temptations: to regard the world as the tragedy of the meaningless. And hence the Christian optimism of the incarnation, persisting even on the cross, means something which man is of himself incapable of achieving, and can indeed only achieve *post Christum natum*.

At the same time it is, of course, important to hold on to the truth that Christians can only expect God's sole and ultimate act to give a redemptive outcome to the appalling drama of world history (without any by-passing of death) if they themselves make their own contribution, as a realization and proof of their faith in this eschatological salvation, to the saving and healing of the world, to the maintenance and establishment of its internal structures, to its preservation, if only partial; to the achievement, if only as a fragmentary beginning of it, of the eschatological salvation here and now. Precisely because God has, in the incarnation, taken the world finally to himself, so that it is simply not true that its ultimate beatitude is something merely promised, not performed; precisely because it is true that it is in so far as he has already come that the Lord is he who is to come, it is not possible for a Christian's attitude and activity to consist simply in waiting for salvation as a gift from God, standing by as an idle spectator while the natural order disintegrates and the world proves its incapability of achieving its own fulfilment by its own power.

True though it is that the world's history has already brought it to the point of discovering, in an ultimately eschatological sense, its ultimate and indestructible unity, this unity is nevertheless still unconsummated. It is unconsummated in us and in our world in which we live. Unconsummated in us, since we are still striving towards the total integration of our whole nature into the grace and love of God, still yearning for the glory of the children of God. Unconsummated in the world, since here too the natural spheres are not yet finally integrated into the grace of God in Christ, because the world is still in a state of sinful confusion, is not yet the transfigured embodiment of grace. The fact that it is thus unconsummated, though the only remedy for it, which the world has no power to bring about, is the coming of God in the second coming of Christ, nevertheless represents a task for us. If (or since) man's ultimate spiritual attitudes (man being essentially of this world)

can be realized only in bodily action in the world, then his incarnational faith in the event, which has already happened
but remains hidden, of the final salvation of the world in the
incarnation and resurrection of Christ can be truly realized
only in human action in and upon the world, not in any purely
idealistic sentiment whether of the whole man or of his interior
mind.

But an act of faith of this kind in the world as taken to
himself by God and sharing in the divine order, an act which
must express itself in relation to the world itself, can be
thought of in only two ways, which are themselves intimately
related one to another and must, fundamentally, achieve a
unity in every Christian life. Either it is an act of faith in
there being grace for the world, not under the control of
man's efforts made while surrendering some positive, relatively significant aspect of the world, relatively rich in the
promise of happiness, which is given up to express the belief
that real salvation is not of this world though it is for the
world: i.e. an act of asceticism. Or else it is an act of positive healing action towards the world, an act of protection
towards the world despite the doom of death laid upon it,
i.e. an act of affirmation towards the world which, because it
neither flees from the world in Buddhist renunciation nor
sees it in a utopian dazzle, can be, as much as the other, an
act of faith in that glory which God confers upon the world
and has already imparted to it in Christ.

This unity of the orders of redemption and creation, still
unconsummated and hence a task for us, to be met with either
the ascetic or the affirmative act of faith, still, because it still
awaits consummation, retains its vulnerability. Neither in his
ascesis nor in his affirmation of the world can the Christian
take up an attitude based on the idea either that the world is,
in an absolute sense, in a state of tragic dissolution or that it
is already, in all its individual aspects, in a state of final reconciliation. He cannot (even by following the evangelical

counsels) simply flee from the world as though it were merely unredeemed and doomed to destruction, able to contribute nothing to his salvation except as something to flee from, see through and renounce as non-being. But nor can he ever feel called upon to construct and control the world in such a way as would suppose that the construction could ever have, within the limits of this world's historical experience, an absolute success; that ultimate success—the transfiguration of the world and man's beatitude—could be achieved, utopian fashion, by forces inherent in the world and under man's control; as though it were not the case that everything man does in his life and in the world is required to undergo that total placing in jeopardy, that absolute surrender which we call death, both in its individual and its cosmic significance.

But because man is, on the one hand, saddled with the work of manifesting the unity of the created and redemptive orders as his task, though one which he cannot fully carry out, and is also, on the other hand, in constant danger of misunderstanding this task in terms either of anti-worldly pessimism or of worldly optimism, it follows that the fulfilment of the task, and hence the unity of the two orders as something to be consummated through men, is itself permanently threatened. True, the danger is as a whole already met and forestalled by the eschatological victory of God's grace in its irrevocable and indestructible acceptance of the world. But within the space and time which lie between the initiation of that victory in Christ's incarnation and resurrection and its manifestation in his second coming, there is for individual men, individual people, and even for the Church, a history of free decision which is still, for them, an open question; and hence there can still be, within that history, both victories and defeats in the achievement of their task, which is the bringing forth of this unity.

A Christian may, on the one hand, let this unity fall below the level of intensity attainable at any given moment by forgetting his Christian sobriety in a utopian intoxication with the world, forgetting his supernatural vocation, which is not simply identical with his duty towards the world, and hence overrating the potentialities of this world at its own level and trying prematurely and violently to impose a consummation on it in his own age; which is the very way to make the unity of the created and redemptive orders fall short of whatever degree of intensity is possible for it at the moment, and so to cause both suffering and supernatural damage to himself.

On the other hand, he may not seriously believe that the world, despite the bad state it is in, is and remains God's and Christ's world, and can even now, if only tentatively and symbolically, participate in beatitude and redemption. So he retires into the ghetto and surrenders his responsibility, assuming an individualistic and fundamentally petty-bourgeois attitude which sees Christianity as the religion of the losing side; he lets the world fall, by default, into the hands of powers and forces inimical to God and Christ, and so lets the unity of the created and redemptive orders fall short of that degree of intensity which it might at that moment have reached. It is a unity which is constantly in danger.

For the same reason, it is a hidden unity. That is to say that the order of redemption, as a whole, is in the first place an object of faith; despite the fact that the redemptive order does manifest itself in wonders and signs of the power of the Spirit, faith must affirm it as not simply accessible to experience and hence as something hidden. The unity is further hidden in that God's grace, with its power to save the world, works for the most part anonymously and can itself be mistaken for one of the forces and potentialities inherent in the world. And it is further hidden in that it is always required to traverse the scandal of the Cross: that is, it is always contradicted by the fact that the world is not saved, that every heroic effort to improve it seems always to come once more tragically *ad absurdum* and to produce out of itself the very things that will destroy its success; so that the world seems always to present itself as an absurd, never-achievable adventure whose only truly and realistically demonstrable outcome is death. In other words: The redemptive order itself is hidden in the darkness of faith, its power over the world is always subject to misinterpretation as a power immanent in the world, and furthermore never seems, even when it is recognized as divine power, to achieve anything final in the world but seems subject to the world's own stronger law, the law of dissolution and death. The unity of the created and redemptive orders is hidden, and its very hiddenness represents a danger to its fulfilment.

These peculiarities in the unity between the redemptive and created orders as history goes on its way imply (let us add at this point) a peculiar attitude on the part of Christians towards the world, and this again is an almost infallible criterion for valid Christianity: namely, a realistic sobriety on the part of Christians about the world, such as, fundamentally, only Christians can have (whether they explicitly know about their own Christianity or are purely anonymous Christians, i.e. men in a state of God's justifying grace). A Christian can never divinize the world. For all its splendor and its unfathomable depths, it can never, for him, be really numinous, but only God's creation, suspended over the abyss of nothingness. The Christian also takes a sober view of the world in that he can never think, whether in theory or practice, that it contains within its own being, as an ineradicable part of itself, the power to fulfil itself in any ultimate sense which would preserve it in the end against collapsing into meaningless perdition. The Christian knows that the only truly attainable ultimate consummation of the world, even though it is realized in the world through his own decisions and acts, is nevertheless given solely by God's act alone. It comes from above, and is not merely the product of a development immanent in the world and in history. Hence this consummation, from which alone everything else receives its ultimate meaning, cannot be forcibly attained by man but is given at just that point where man has to all appearances merely reached the ultimate depths of his impotence. The Christian knows that he will constantly be sent by God upon courses which he cannot by himself complete; that tasks will be laid upon him which cannot be finally performed while the fashion of this world remains; that he has always to fight, without, as yet, being able to see any final victory, indeed that it would be a danger signal of the most appalling defeat if he so much as wanted to fight in such fashion as to achieve a once-for-all victory.

And yet the Christian does not despair of this world. He works, he keeps on beginning again, he does not give up. He is sceptical about the permanence of his concrete Christian imperatives and is always prepared, when taught by fresh experience, to revise them; yet he has the courage to apply them and propagate them, without supposing that they are the final solution of all the problems of concrete living. To speak in scriptural terms, he is a man who by faith knows and loves the "endurance" of hope, awaiting its fulfilment from God alone. This mean between utopianism and despair, which can never be unambiguously and rigorously justified, is of all the miracles of God's grace the most prosaic, seeming almost like mere crude insensitivity. For not to despair of the world without help from the analgesic of secular optimism is always, even when it seems to happen as a matter of course, as the mere modest common sense of an honest man endowed with grace and constancy, a triumph of the grace of God. We can test ourselves by it to know whether we are being really Christian.

II. Application to Christian Living

What is implied by all this, if we now ask what sort of look a Christian life must have if the formative influence in it is this unity of the redemptive and created orders as it now is—actual, yet differentiated, real, eschatologically revealed even now, but still a task to be realized, still unconsummated, still vulnerable, still hidden? We must say something about this question. But what can be said about it here and now can obviously only suggest a preliminary sketch of how the theological considerations we have made here are to be applied.

1. First of all, what has been said already makes it possible for us to understand the unity and the distinction between secular status and the status of the evangelical counsels. If both are to imply a realization of Christian life—and, in both cases, basically, of Christian life in all its consummated fullness—then it is clear that it is not permissible for secular status to involve either a degree of indifference towards the redemptive order or a practical identification of the two orders without distinction or qualification; nor is it permissible for the status of the counsels to be regarded as so committed to the redemptive order as to have no further task in the world. For each status, the unity of the two orders as distinct from each other, and as a unity as yet unconsummated and vulnerable, remains a permanent task. The secular Christian cannot attend to the world as though he had found God when all he has done is to be true to the world, for this would mean that the created order is already simply identical with the redemptive order. But this would be a heresy, not something that follows from the real unity between the two orders. Even the Christian in the world must always be something more than a man working at the immanent tasks of the world and humanity. His relationship with God cannot be adequately mediated simply through the world and its fulfilment. A man acting competently in the world and the affairs of life is not, so far, simply a Christian, true though it is that a really valid and human competence in these matters is indeed an element, if only implicit, in being Christian. The secular Christian too,

by prayer, by self-denial, by sharing in the Church's life in
the narrower sense, by an acceptance, in faith, hope, patience
and humility, of the failures which beset the world, must work
for the realization of the redemptive order as something
which, even though it integrates the created order into itself,
nevertheless surpasses it.

On the other hand, the Christian following the evangelical
counsels, the man dedicated to asceticism and the renunciation of the world, has a positive task in respect of the world,
because he cannot accept and realize the redemptive order
unless he also carries out that descent of grace into the world
which has been accomplished in the incarnation and resurrection of Christ. It is, equally, impermissible to him to think
that his renunciation of the world, which can never, fundamentally, be anything more than relative, could, as such,
compel the grace of God; as though, in the living of eternal
life, as the world goes down God necessarily goes up. He
too must ask himself where his contribution comes in to
the healing and sanctifying of the world and the growth in
unity of the two orders. The contribution can, in the concrete,
take many different forms. It does not necessarily have to
consist in the employment in cultural or directly apostolic
work of the human energies set free by the renunciation
embodied in the counsels. The example set by a contemplative
flight from the world, if it is humble and truly recognizes
the Christian in the world as equally justified, can be such
a contribution; for the Church's power of fulfilling, in her
lay Christians, the worldly task of transforming the world
can only be maintained if these laymen are truly seeking God
above and beyond everything in the world and through and
beyond all its failures. It is only when a Christian with the
status of the counsels is aware of the commandment to love
his neighbor, and through that of his responsibility for the
world, so that he takes his place in the whole mission of the

Church to intensify the unity of the two orders, that he is really a Christian.

Hence men of either status will be living, equally, according to the differentiated unity of the two orders. The distinction between one status and the other can and may and must come about only because the act of faith in that unity, which is also an act of love and hope, can be realized either through a partial renunciation of the world or through an acceptance of the world despite the doom of death laid upon it; for the totality of what the Church does and is required to do is allotted and articulated in various functions amongst her individual members, within her abiding unity, according to the disposition of her Spirit; and the whole can still be present in each allotted function, without prejudice to its special character.

2. We said at the beginning of the theological discussion that Christian life and ecclesial life are not actually identical. There is an area in which Christianity, the supernatural, elevating, sanctifying grace of God, is given its realization in the world, and which is not directly governed and directed by any commands or rulings given by the Church in her teaching and pastoral office. But this non-ecclesial, non-hierarchical sphere is not simply the sphere of the merely secular, in the sense of being irrelevant to a man's supernatural salvation and to the healing and sanctification of the world. We can illustrate this with some simple examples.

No one can be authoritatively told by his ecclesiastical superior whether to become a doctor or an actor, but the circumstances may be such that this decision may determine not only the temporal and external welfare of the individual in question but much else, for good or ill, in his environment in the world and in the Church. In the political sphere, the Church can indeed pass judgment on some particular economic or social measure to the extent of deciding whether it accords with her fundamental norms in this field; but she cannot officially determine, with final and unambiguous authority, whether or not this set of quite concrete guiding principles is really, here and now, the most appropriate and practical way of achieving the social and political goal at which we are bound to aim. Yet here again is something which could have incalculable effects for good or ill on the world. Nor do we mean that a choice between two courses both lying within the framework of the Church's norms must be morally indifferent, merely because the Church in her teaching and pastoral office is not in a position to give the individual making the choice clear instructions on which alternative is the practically right one and hence (often) the only morally right one too. It is perfectly possible for the individual to realize on quite other grounds than that of an ecclesiastical or doctrinal decision what course is, here and now, not only practical but also, for him, the only responsible and moral course in the circumstances. Such choices, and the very act of distinguishing them from other cases, thus embody a moral and hence supernaturally significant decision which cannot be called ecclesial nor attributed, as a concrete act, to the influence of the Church in her official capacity.

There is, then, such a thing as Christian life as distinct from strictly ecclesial life: not only because there are Christians who are not Catholics and nevertheless possess sanctifying grace and the acts that flow from it, but also because Christians and ecclesial life are not simply identical in the members of the Catholic Church herself; what is ecclesial represents only a part of what is Christian, and the latter, even where it is not strictly ecclesial, is supernaturally relevant to the salvation of the individual and, above all, to the salvation and sanctification of the world. However much we may value and promote the importance, and even in certain circumstances the obligation, of participation by the laity in ecclesial life, especially in supporting and facilitating the strictly hierarchical apostolate, however much we may propose this to the laity and impress it upon them, it yet remains true that the lay Christian has his rightful, primary and absolutely inalienable task in the field of strictly non-ecclesial but nevertheless essentially Christian activity. The apostolate which belongs primarily to the lay Christian is precisely that in which he exercises responsibility for the world in those areas in which, in the nature of the case, the hierarchically constituted Church cannot do so as part of her office.

Here too the layman is a member of the Church, for it is precisely the power of truth, of holiness, of grace residing ultimately in the Church which he, instructed and guided by the Church's proclamation of her norms, is bringing to realization in the world. To this extent, this most strictly lay apostolate too has its roots in the Church's order of reality. But it is not for this reason the apostolate of the Church in the strict sense. It seems to me that everything depends on the layman's understanding that he is, as an individual, irreplaceable, with a specifically Christian and moral task to be performed within groups not directly subject to the Church's official control, a task of which he will have to give an account before the judgment seat of God, even if failure to do his duty in this field never brings him into conflict with the official authority of the Church.

3. What has already been said really includes what needs essentially to be said about the sanctification of the world. Given a right understanding of our theoretical considerations, it must have become clear that the sanctification of the world does not begin at the point where we take a sound and well-developed world with sound and well-developed structures of its own and then impose a supernatural and religious superstructure upon it. There also has to be an explicit, conscious relating of secular affairs to the supernatural salvation which is in Christ, manifested in morality, in custom, in institutions, in a uniting of secular with explicitly religious matters. A Christian can never be content with having a more

or less chemically pure profane world and simply being a Christian too, "on the side" (on Sundays, in church, etc.). Specifically Christian life must come into action in that same sphere of the external material world in which the secular, profane life of this world has its activity.

This is still true even if we ought to be perhaps more readily aware than in ecclesiastical circles we are apt to be that the sphere of the worldly, profane and temporal has today, by the will of God, achieved such a degree of development, extension and complexity that it cannot be given a Christian stamp to that obvious extent which was possible in the simpler time of the Middle Ages or even in the period of Baroque culture. A woman baking her bread at home could trace the sign of the cross on each loaf she made. This does not mean that a modern bakery should be expected to do the same simply because its owners and workers should, ideally speaking, be Christians. We are not to expect, nor even to desire, that the same percentage of total book production should be religious as was the case as late as the eighteenth century, when ninety percent of titles were theological in character. We are going to find in our age that the world of the purely profane has a density, an inevitability, an almost total impenetrability which simply have to be realistically accepted by Christians as a danger, a challenge, and indeed as a positive opportunity; for this merely profane world itself, with its harsh inhumanity and its weight of weariness, may, as time goes on, become a stronger provocation of yearning for a world that is God's world than ever existed in an age when heaven and earth seemed, perhaps all too naively, to be already reconciled.

But while it is true that explicit Christianity must be given its expression in the world itself, must be present in a discernible way (though it is never possible to prescribe, compulsorily, any particular dosage of the secular and profane element in this one world, nor to say that the optimum

opportunity for the salvation of the individual and the sanctification of the world always and at every moment involves
the highest possible percentage of explicit Christianity), yet
what we need above all to say and to appreciate is that the
presence of Christianity and its grace does not stop at the
point where outward expression of explicitly Christian and
ecclesiastical life stops. In order to see this more clearly we
have only to consider that, in practice, to carry out the
natural moral law over the whole field of human existence
and throughout the course of human history, individual and
social, is possible only by God's grace in Christ; so that here
God himself has set up a point of interference between the
heavenly and earthly orders. The Christian and the man in
this world do not each possess their clearly distinct mansion
within the House of God, but each must fulfil his life within
the same sphere of being and using precisely the same material.
What must also be considered is that the natural moral law
is not something extra, superimposed on the norms inherent
in reality, but is the expression of these norms (if only in their
general structure) as something to be respected according to
the will of God; so that a right relationship to persons and to
reality in general is materially identical with the moral norm.
But this unequivocally implies that the Christian healing and
hallowing of this world by God's grace begins at a point
where it would seem, looking from below and at first glance,
as though nothing is happening except a genuine respect for
the real order of things immanent in this world, in so far as
this order is at man's free disposal and subjected to him.

In simple terms: Wherever in this world of men, in its
economic life, in the down-to-earth reality and not merely
the ideal theory of its organized community life, in the whole
length and breadth of individual and social life, right actions
are performed, according to reality, and decency, and humanity, there Christianity is achieved, even if not by that
name, whether by acknowledged Christians or by others acting

in this way; and hence the strictly Christian task of Christians and especially of lay Christians is fulfilled. This is not all that God demands of Christians, but it is something which he demands of them as Christians and not merely as human beings; and it is the most essential element in the healing and sanctifying of the world as such, since the world, in this present phase of the still unconsummated and hidden unity of the redemptive and created orders, can be regarded as almost sufficiently Christianized and "hallowed" if its own order of things merely avoids making the Christian's life any harder for him than (being still in the state of waiting for its share in Christ's resurrection) it inevitably must.

4. This also implies that for a Christian in the world, the experience that he constantly has of the world's need for healing is, in itself, a summons to his specifically Christian task and duty. We must always be clearly aware that it is neither the task nor indeed within the scope of a Christian, least of all a lay Christian, to lay down a supernaturally *a priori* track, as it were, for his whole life, with the faith as starting-point. All that he is and does must indeed be brought face to face with the supernatural principles of his faith and remain under their dominion. But it would not be Christianity, only pseudo-Christian utopianism, to suppose that a Christian could do everything that he does in his life in this world from sheerly supernatural impulses and guiding rules. When a man sets out to become a Christian he finds himself already in a world of experience. Fideism, the denial that there is any primal knowledge in man preceding faith, is a heresy not only in theory but also in practice, which is where it is often attempted. Human beings love other human beings before they come face to face with their task, as Christians, of integrating this love, positively, into their life as Christians; nor are they likely, except in the rarest cases, to begin loving anyone in the first place because they love God and as an actualization of that love. The world and grace are both given

initially, in their original plurality, before we are confronted with the task of realizing their hidden and as yet unconsummated unity.

An untroubled and confident acceptance of this dualism is an essential element in the attitude of a Christian, and especially of a layman. He has to trust, and build on the trust, that his two designs for living, the earthly and heavenly, which are for him, in the first instance, distinct, and which cannot, from his point of view, be deduced one from another, do have an ultimate congruity with each other, hidden in God and solely under the control of his providence, because they are both rooted in the aboriginal unity, differentiated but real, of the redemptive and created orders. But for this very reason it is of the highest importance to see that a Christian may receive a summons to his heavenly task precisely in that area and at that time in which he is devoting himself to the world and its tasks.

Such a summons, transcending the world itself, coming from and leading to the God of supernatural life, can of course make itself heard through what is positive in the world, if heart and hearing are open to it. That measureless demand which grace, active in nature, arouses in the world for a fulfilment which shall complete all that is positive in it and yet go beyond all its possibilities; that insatiable desire for a joy without bounds, a life no longer ruled by death, a personal intimacy not subject to distance—all these, and much besides, are messages of grace coming to men out of the midst of the world and the experience of all that is positive in it. But for sinful man in this age of the world, his ears almost closed to the grace of God, there is another appeal which comes to him (within the area of his specific task and responsibility), coming from the midst of the world itself, and which is more intelligible and more powerful: The experience of the need for salvation which this earthly world bears in itself; the direct experience of its tragic confusion, its subjection to death, the ever-recurring ruin of even the best of human efforts, the baffling dialectic of its very being, in which what is good seems always to stimulate evil, and what is abominable to call forth what is good—all this amounts to a question confronting man, the one which least easily remains unheard, asking him whether he does indeed wish to suppose that he is capable, on his own, of bringing this world to fulfilment.

The experience of the world as we know it in its frustration and its need for salvation can be received and understood as a summons to a Christian interpretation and mastery of the world. A man could come through experience of the world, rightly understood and declining neither into utopianism nor despair, and, after entering in full confidence into that experience, encounter Christianity as showing to the created order as it actually is, in all its frustration and need of salvation, the way towards the higher order of redemption. It would be a good thing if direction in the spiritual life given to lay people were to take more explicit account of this possibility, which is obvious enough in itself. It may be, indeed it is certain, that it is possible to read the message of Jesus Christ with any clarity and fullness in the book of the world only if it has first been read in the book of the Scriptures. But after that it can and should be read in the book of the world and of man's life as well, so that what is said in the book of the Scriptures may be truly understood; the life of the world, if only it is experienced in its wholeness and without reserve, is itself a part of the spiritual life, and above all in its experience of the world's dire need of salvation.

5. The theoretical discussion will also have made it clear how we are to look at the actual situation of the lay Christian and his activity in the world. It was there established that we can regard the world, precisely in its actual worldliness, distinct from grace and redemption, as a presupposition of the redemptive order, and even as a factor within it. The

point is that the higher order itself establishes the lower as its own presupposition, different from and really lower than itself, in such fashion that the lower, while fully retaining its real and abiding difference, has no need to fall away from its unity with the higher order. This puts us in a position to make a right evaluation of the much-deplored gap which so often appears between the attitude of many Christians and the appropriate course of action in a given situation. A Christian attitude on the one hand and an appropriate course of action within the framework of this world on the other are two really distinct factors within a totality whose consummated unity is a task still awaiting fulfilment. In so far as these two factors are distinct, there is no guarantee that a Christian's attitude will embrace whatever course of action is appropriate to the worldly situation; the Christian view may be "well-meaning," but nevertheless inappropriate as action; yet the two things cannot be simply divided one from another. A Christian attitude is only fully and completely itself when it sets up an appropriate course of action as distinct from and presupposed to itself, while continuing to maintain it in unity with itself; and appropriate action takes shape in the concrete order when it gives its own dynamism its full scope while continuing to stand in need of the grace of God and also of a Christian attitude of mind, whether conscious or implicit.

A completely Christian attitude, even when operating in an area not directly under the authority of the Church in her official capacity, does necessarily involve appropriate action as well; it is an attitude which desires to redeem the structures immanent in the world, in the created order, for the sake of their own sanctification and fulfilment, and by this very means it creates the necessary basis for its own fulfilment. So long as this unity between appropriate action and Christian attitudes is still only on the way to fulfilment, as is the case with the whole unity between the redemptive and created orders, Christians

must bear with a certain discrepancy between the two as a
burden laid upon them and a share in the Cross of Christ.

6. What we have said has established that there is a unity
and a distinction between the Church in her official aspect
and the Church of Christians regarded as men having a task
in the world. The two, while keeping their difference from
each other, have a true unity which must be maintained but
not misunderstood as a simple identity. Perhaps this may
make it possible to determine theologically the true significance of Catholic diocesan organizations and Catholic Action
generally. They might take their natural stand at that point
where the unity between the created and redemptive orders,
with their abiding difference, offers itself palpably as a task
that is not yet completed. For there must be a concrete point
of contact in the Church by which the powers of truth and
grace belonging to the redemptive order, so far as the Church
disposes of them, are imparted to Christians at precisely that
point where they, in their worldly office, no longer strictly
ecclesial but still essentially Christian, bear these powers out
into the world to heal and sanctify it. And there must, on
the other hand, be a concrete point of contact in the world
by which Christians in the world can bring that world as
they experience and suffer it, the world which is subject to
them themselves and not directly to the hierarchy, and offer
it to the grace of God in the Church; so that this healed and
sanctified created order can become, with all the more fullness
and purity, a constituent of the redemptive order as it is made
manifest within the Church.

There has of course always, in all ages, been such a point
of contact in the Church for mediating this unity, still seeking
its way to fulfilment, between the redemptive and created
orders; it has always existed, whether or not it has had any
corporate organization or even any name. But in an age in
which the world (which man does not merely discover, but
creates for himself) has reached such a degree of richness,

variety and deadly peril as our age, the task of finding the way to greater unity has become immeasurably huge; it needs special organizational means and materials. The difficulty of preserving a clear, calm, sober Christian realism between despair and utopianism, neither losing, in pseudo-Christian worldly activism, our unqualified faith that even failure and disaster can, for him who has fought with honor, be a true victory, nor, on grounds of its imperfectibility or its failures, dispensing ourselves from fidelity to a constantly renewed responsibility for the world—in such a world as ours, this difficulty too has grown to immense proportions. Nevertheless, this difficulty is not so great as the power of God's grace for one who believes that, whether in life or in death, we are the Lord's, and that it is only through both and in a fashion that is ultimately in God's hand alone, that the blessed final unity between the order of redemption and the order of creation can be achieved.

3

THE SIGNIFICANCE IN REDEMPTIVE HISTORY OF THE INDIVIDUAL MEMBER OF THE CHURCH

Only a very naive optimist would expect here anything more than a few observations in connection with the title theme. To say more would involve writing a complete ontology of man and a complete theology. We must ask the reader, right from the start, to bear this inescapable limitation of treatment in mind, if it should happen that he fails to find here the very things he would have expected on this subject.

I. Ontology of the Relationship between Individuality and Community

If we are to say anything about the individual and his significance to the Church in terms of redemptive history, we must necessarily begin with what is meant by this "individual." But this is very difficult; for it is impossible to establish any single, unambiguous meaning for the word. It stands for an "analogical" concept, i.e. one whose content includes within itself a certain variability in what it stands for, and can be embodied in very different forms, though this does not make it possible to distinguish clearly between the concept and the form in which its content is embodied. Thus, *individual* may mean no more than one of a series of equivalents, differentiated only quantitatively and spatially within a homogeneous mass. Here every individual equals every other, the value of each

is only a matter of its position, they are interchangeable and
—unimportant. Each can be replaced by any other, and its
sole significance lies in the fact that it contributes, purely
quantitatively, to making the whole bigger than it would
be without that individual; a contribution, moreover, by
which the only real increase is in the sheer *mass* of the whole.

But even so there is something mysterious here for metaphysical wonderment: the one is not the other and yet they
belong together, are interrelated and in some sense *"for* one
another"; neither would be what it is if it were not for the
other. We do not propose to go into the question of whether
there can in point of fact be, even in the world of physics
(or indeed of mathematics), an "individual" which is individual only in this sense: differentiated only by its position in an
absolutely homogeneous mass. Perhaps in fact there cannot
be any such thing; perhaps the very word "position" is an
indication that there is no such thing, but that such a notion
of individuality is merely a sort of lower limit; that even
each ultimate infinitesimal physical particle has something
about it which differentiates it, even as to content, from
every other one, so that there simply cannot (thank God?) be
such a thing as an absolutely homogeneous mass, and hence
nothing can ever be simply and adequately replaced by anything else that exists.

However that may be, there certainly are not *only* individuals in the sense that we have seen so far. If we simply cannot
suppose anything, even in thought, without attributing to it
at least a "position," so as to have something about it which
other things have not got, by which it can be distinguished
from others (if only a particular place in imaginary space),
this fact shows that even at this lowest level of possible thought
the meaning and content of the concept "individual" include
a dynamic openness pointing towards another, intensified,
embodiment of it. This is not the place to trace the variations
of the concept through all the levels of being up to its full

expression—e.g. to inquire how it applies at the organic level. We will turn immediately to consider the individual as it exists at the level where person, spirit, and the possession of oneself in self-consciousness and free choice set their stamp on individuality as such.

There can be no doubt that the thinking person is a "separate individual" in a sense which cannot hold good for anything that is not present to itself. The subhuman individual is constituted in a way which needs to be precisely and clearly seen if anything is to be understood of the problem involved in this question: namely, its difference from and its bond with what is other than itself increase and decrease together. This seems at first to be a contradiction. At first sight one is inclined to say that anything that exists possesses its own peculiarity (and difference) in inverse ratio to its unity with, its bond with, what is other than itself; that, in other words, it decreases in selfhood the more it becomes bound up with something else, while any growth in distinguishing selfhood involves a decrease in its unity with and relationship to anything other than itself. It is no exaggeration to say that this error, seemingly such a self-evident truth, the apparent contradition between all-embracing unity and individual uniqueness, lies at the root of all the errors and heresies that have arisen in the study of relationships, of "social being." And yet even at the lowest subhuman level, if we look at it properly, we see that it is not so. Something that is merely separated spatially and temporally from something else is neither really anything for itself (does not really possess anything for itself) nor really one with anything else. Empty bits of space and time are precisely as empty as they are separate from each other: separate from each other, yet not present to themselves, merely parts of the whole and yet not really united with it. Hence the true law of things is not: the more special and distinct in character, the more separated, isolated and discontinuous from everything else, but the reverse: the more really special a thing is, the more abundance of being it has in itself, the more intimate unity and mutual participation there will be between it and what is other than itself.

When we speak of "individuals," by an almost constitutionally faulty tendency in human thought to make visual images of things (thanks to its bias towards spatio-temporal sense-observation), we are impelled to think about spatial extension, spatial series, portions of a mass, numerical position, something that can be counted, something that has plenty more of the same sort in, in principle, unlimited numbers along with it. And then, almost inevitably, we miss the real meaning of the individual. For the individual (we return here once more to the dimension of person and mind) is not characterized, primarily, by having others of the same sort "along with" it, by being inserted in a mass of others of the same kind and then somehow divided off from them (*how,* ultimately, once having got as far as this?). God too is a "single individual"; so much so that to acknowledge the one God is part of the foundation of Christian belief and of all true belief in God. But he is not an individual by having others beside him, so that to name him would be to begin the counting of a series. He is one, single and individual precisely by being unsurpassably all-embracing, excluding nothing from himself; one, not by differentiation from and amongst many others (so that the whole lot might be in some way counted together), but one by infinity. If finite individuals, as distinct from God, do have other individuals "along with" them, yet this distinguishing "along with" needs to be rightly understood. It cannot be eliminated, if we want to imagine what we mean by "individual"; what we have already described as our constitutional tendency towards confusion cannot be avoided; but it must be cancelled out even in the very moment of applying it. For wherever we have mind and person, there (as the philosophers say) is transcendence towards infinity; and the individual and separate, the finite and defined, are known in the act in which the intellectually knowing subject opens itself to the boundless and infinite.

In the apprehending of what goes beyond apprehension we perceive something which exists alongside something else; only in that same act of apprehension the knowing subject turns "back on itself" and realizes that it itself is that "individual." And this holds not only for spirit as knowledge, but for spirit as love. The self-bestowal of the spirit in love, desire, self-surrender (whether we call it will, love, longing, delight or anything else) always involves an opening of itself to infinity, a reaching out beyond all limitations towards God, beside whom there is nothing because he is the perfect fullness of all actuality. True knowledge of the true individuality of a spiritual person (such knowledge being itself a constitutive factor in such individuality) thus takes place in a spiritual, loving opening of oneself to the all-embracing being: that which has nothing beside itself because it includes everything. And hence true spiritual individuality is not the opposite of unity with everything else and with the whole (it is knowledge and love which make true unity; the knower and the known, the lover and the beloved are more truly one than, say, what is connected according to physical laws, as being subject to the same field, etc.). For this individuality and the relationship binding it to everything else are actually constituted and come into existence by the act in which the spiritual subject opens itself, in knowledge and love, to that limitless and all-embracing being whom we call God.

Of course this transcendent openness, which at one and the same time, and in the same degree, both makes one and individualizes, may exist in a man merely as the essential structure of his spirit, verified in all his personal acts whether by affirmation or free denial; or on the other hand it may be freely and lovingly accepted by him as his essential structure, i.e. in such fashion that he wills to be what he inescapably is: himself, and at the same time never an isolated monad; himself in so far as he communicates with all things and in so far as everything other than himself, as such, conditions his own inner peculiar selfhood. This basic structure (which is man's essence and nature), in which individuality and community are complementary and not contrary to each other, can exist and develop within the context of acceptance or within the context of denial and protest. Hence, because of that constitutional mistake which we mentioned before, a man may think either that he can escape from himself by flight into the collective, or that he can be and become a separate individual by solipsistically cutting himself off from any surrender by knowledge and love to that which is greater and more all-embracing than he is on his own (whereas he would, in his way, become "everything" himself in a true sense if he willingly, openly, gave himself to that every-ready Openness).

This twofold misconception of one's own nature by a combination of fear and *hubris* (fearing either one's own uniqueness or the all-embracing greater being, and at the same time making it into an absolute) brings us to the following point: one can only make this existential mistake of thinking that one must, or indeed can, choose between individuality and collectivity if there is at least some appearance of opposition between them. But this only happens, in the concrete, when we are not dealing with these directly complementary entities as related to each other at the same level of being. These two formally polarized concepts are then contrasted as they exist at two different levels of reality, and here of course they are opposed to each other, not as individuality to universality but as structures belonging to different strata and grades of reality. In more concrete terms: community at the biological level of the preservation of the species is not opposed to individuality as found at this level; the member of the pack or herd finds itself as an individual precisely in its membership.

The individuality of the spiritual person is not opposed to the loving community of persons; each can, essentially, be itself only through the other. But spiritual, personal individuality can be really in opposition (which does not immediately involve contradiction) to community at the social biological level, at the material physical level, at the level of organization, etc. So it may happen, for instance, that in the name of spiritual, personal freedom someone liberalistically or anarchistically rejects social collectivity, seeing it as a threat; or, conversely, that he tries to eliminate spiritual, personal individuality in favor of community at a lower level of being. A real problem of mutual tension between individual and universal thus arises only when, in the stratified plurality of human existence, there has to be an adjustment between a personality (or community) at one particular human level (e.g. economics, the state, the Church) and a community (or personality) at another level. Because man is, in himself, this plural reality, it is his valid, and difficult, task to effect a reconciliation of individual and universal at the different levels of his own being. But the problem which arises from this deceptive appearance of things to which we have referred, the problem to which he constantly succumbs and which drives him to insoluble conflicts and extremes, is posed by setting up one side of these two correlated concepts, at one level of reality, in an absolute opposition to the other side of it as found at another level.

Already (to anticipate the subject with which we are actually going to deal) we have a glimpse of the real, relevant way to state the problem we are considering. The individual in the dimension of the spiritual and personal and of supernatural grace is not opposed to and does not constitute any threat to the community in that same dimension: the community of the objective Spirit, of the Church in so far as she is the community of those joined together in the Holy Spirit and made one in interior faith and the love which is a gift of grace. But a problem does indeed arise about how the individual who, existing as a spiritual-personal and pneumatic being—i.e. at the highest level of individuality—can at the same time be a member of the Church which, because it also exists as a society with a physical, biological foundation and an outward organization, is not only a community of spiritual personalities and of the Holy Spirit but also an institutional and legally organized society. What needs to be seen in this connection is that a man and a Christian must not make either of these valid and really existing opposites into an absolute, on either side. So long as he is on pilgrimage in this world of time, he must maintain the relative opposition between them; he must know that he is dealing here with an opposition between a higher and a lower level, and be clear, in all his handling of it, about which pole is to be given priority in case of doubt or of having to choose, which side of the tension is, in any particular historical situation, in greater danger and hence in need of special safeguards. But we are anticipating the development of our argument.

II. The Individual in the Order of Grace and the Church

Before we can go any further into this problem, we first need to say, explicitly, that the individual endowed with supernatural grace is the highest and most radical example of individuality among all created things; and that the fulfilment of this individuality is in fact what the Church is there to serve, in relation to which she, as a social, external and legal institution, is the lower and hence the subordinate thing.

Our starting-point is the spiritual-personal individual. We need once more to state here explicitly that man is such a thing, because this is the *potentia obedientialis* for what we are going to call the grace-endowed supernatural individual. Simply as a spiritual person, present to himself and freely disposing of himself, man is no mere particular instance of the universal. He is unique and can never, ultimately, be wholly derived from anything else; his individuality in being what he is, is not merely a negatively spatio-temporal nailing down of the universal idea, into a particular here-and-now situation. Because man is an individual in this sense, because he is never merely one exemplification of a general idea, never merely an instance of a type, he has a valid existence whose reality is not identical with his space-time existence; he is "immortal," the subject of an eternal choice and an eternal destiny.

It necessarily follows from what has been said already that it is given to this spiritual-personal individuality to have an entirely special sort of community (community of minds in truth and in the objective goods of culture such as art, etc., and community of really personal love, "thou" to "thou"). There follows, equally, the inseparable connection of these two with one another, as two sides of one and the same level of being. But man in the supernatural order, which is the direct self-communication of God in the grace of Christ, is, even as regards his individuality, something more than this merely spiritual-personal subject with its correlated community of truth and love. For if the concept of individuality is an analogical concept, a transcendental characteristic of an existent thing, itself varying according to the level of that thing's being, then it follows that individuality as such will attain a higher degree and a more radical intensity if the thing to which it belongs is raised to a higher ontological order. But this is what happens when man, while keeping his spiritual nature as such, by which he is and remains "man," is raised to the supernatural order. By grace, which means, in the last analysis, God's self-communication to his creature in a quasi-formal causality and not, in the last analysis, a created reality produced by efficient causality, man is in his very being elevated into an order which is essentially higher than that of a merely naturally spiritual person.

This is not the place for a more detailed explanation of why this unique elevation of the spiritual nature of man, in his very being, does not imply the abolition of his essential nature. What makes it possible for his own nature to be thus elevated yet still preserved is that his natural being is capable, because of the limitless transcendence of spirit even at the natural level, of being filled, by grace, with the reality of God himself and thus raised above every creaturely aspiration, without any need to abolish that transcendently infinite horizon which is his "limit," his "definition." But if man thus belongs, though only by the free gift of grace, to a divine order, if he is infinitely more than a man and the spiritual person implied in being a man, then it necessarily follows also that he possesses a grace-given pneumatic individuality. And this individuality excels the natural individuality of the spiritual person to precisely the same degree that the order of grace excels mere nature, however much it goes without saying that nature and its individuality, as the presupposed *potentia obedientialis,* are "assumed" and hence preserved within the supernatural order and the individuality which it confers.

This concept of a grace-given supernatural individuality, at which we have now arrived by considerations of a purely formal ontological and theological nature, needs of course, so far as can here be done, to be filled in with a content of a more concrete kind. When God loves, his love is truly creative. It fully and really makes what is loved into what it is loved as. But when God loves in the supernatural love of an absolute self-communication of his own inner divine life, then this act of his, though it may be formulated in general terms, must nevertheless, if it is to be rightly understood, be seen to be in the highest degree concrete and individual. For the more personal a love is, the more the person himself is committed and surrendered in this love, so much the more individual, unique and irreplaceable does this love become. And this, of course, applies in the most radical sense when God is the lover and this divine love, as God's supernatural self-communication, reaches the absolute, unsurpassable level. In such a case this love can be nothing short of absolutely unique. In this love, then, God cannot possibly be merely manifesting that general benevolence which, as creator, he extends to his creatures, as a benevolent lord and ruler who is "equitable" and "just" towards his subjects. Rather, God must love each one in an essentially new and unique way which is simply not possible within the limits of the created order. Hence it is not strange that this love should be represented and expressed by means of the love which is, in our experience, the most individual and non-interchangeable of all, namely the love of bridegroom and bride, the love of marriage.

But if God's love for the individual man is thus, in each case, divinely unique; if his gift of himself is not something general, as though he were the same for everyone, equally accessible and universally distributed; if God's act of self-communication to the individual man is rather, in each case, a fresh, exceptional, ever unique miracle of utterly personal love, divinely radical and divinely unique—then, through this love, the beloved himself is truly someone absolutely unique. It is indeed true that God has called each one by his name. The order of supernatural grace, strictly as such, allows to the very minimum degree for things to exist as cases, as repetitions, with rules repeatedly applicable in the same way, laws capable of being valid for many. One can say little about it, because it is always something unique, whereas we can only express generality. For expressing what is individual we are given, ultimately, only the dumb, ostensive gesture and the direct experience of our own incommunicable destiny and unspoken love; not speech, which ranges over "generalities." But this is the very reason for there being this pneumatic individual; the individual as he is called forth by God's totally self-giving love. For in this sense too God is infinite love: love that can give itself to each one differently. Not only nor primarily as regards the "degree" of this love, but first and last in the uniquely *special* character of the love which God gives to each one, by which each one becomes, himself, unique. (Perhaps this involves something which comes hard on us during our pilgrimage here through darkness and incomprehensibility: we do not yet see God face to face, and hence we do not as yet comprehend each other. The other is bound to remain an enigma to us if he is God's unique beloved.)

This leads to a further consequence: the free decisions which an individual makes as a spiritual person are not merely (though of course and necessarily they are this too) the fulfilment, by application to a given case, of a central law; they are the realization of a genuinely spiritual personal *and* grace-given, supernatural individuality in obedience to a completely personal call, a genuinely individual vocation from God. And this call is none the less individual, unique and irreplaceable for being, often enough, manifested only through the ordinariness of everyday life and the force of external circumstances, and in a manner that is instinctive rather than reflective. Wherever this spiritual and, above all, supernatural individuality comes fully into play, the spiritual and religious acts expressing the nature of this double individuality become, necessarily, something extremely central. They really proceed from the very heart of the person; they are necessarily something more than the product of training, of imitative behavior, of the mere fulfilment of a general propositional law coming from outside oneself; they go beyond what is to be done on all occasions by everybody, what can be directly preached, prescribed and subjected to control. Of course all such acts are, and have to be, all this as well. They would represent a failure in true, human, spiritual-personal, grace-endowed individuality as willed by God, they would become acts of hubristic solipsis and of an egoism with little, fundamentally, of real individuality about it, if they refused to insert themselves into the full range and many-levelled complexity of human existence. They must submit, in creaturely humility and in that fearless, uninhibited simplicity which does not fear for its own individuality, to all the structures inherent in that many-levelled, complex reality; they must *also* be acts of fulfilment of the law, of subordination to an external society, of respect for what is institutional, customary, moral, etc.; they must *also* lean upon habit, training, lines of association laid down by a physiologically conditioned psychology, etc.

But they are only what they are really meant to be if they are more than all this. They must be acts of what is most intimately basic in man: unforced, unforceable acts of his unique freedom, acts which, of their very nature, cannot be compelled from without by the suggestions and conditioning of education, of so-called public opinion, of advertising, of the imitative instinct, of infection from other psyches, or by "the masses." All these psychological mechanisms exist, and must and should exist, too, in the sphere of man's religious and moral life. For these mechanisms belong to man, and in the religious sphere man is present in his totality. But his religious acts are what they need to be in order to be truly religious only if they are something more than products of these psychological mechanisms, more than the activation of those levels of reality in man which lie outside the real kernel of his spiritual and supernatural individuality.

Of course genuinely religious acts are only such because, and in so far as, they are individual (in the double sense indicated). This *individuality* in such acts is only one distinguishing mark among others (and perhaps not, in fact, even the most important one) by which these acts are characterized. For they must also be really *spiritual* acts. Acts emanating from the center of the person in real freedom and responsibility. Acts which are concerned with God not merely in the sense of their conceptual subject-matter but in their genuinely free affirmation of transcendence, acts determinatively affecting the basic substance of man, acts in which man really commits himself to his own eternal essence and in which that primal mystery which silently governs his being becomes present.

But all this does in fact imply that such an act is also necessarily an individual act in the sense meant here. And conversely, it is only where this individuality wins through that the other characteristics are present without which a human act (however much it may be conscious, free in the merely legal sense, and conceptually concerned with God) is not a genuine and radically religious act. There is a point here which we must not overlook: Because this personal and supernatural individuality and centrality, which are of the essence of real religious acts, are not directly accessible to any external experience nor even, directly, to any interior one which works by reflection and objectivization, there is a constant possibility and danger of mistaking for such acts those others which arise, basically, only at the pre-personal level but, to a superficial diagnosis, nevertheless look like real religious acts. One need only have understood the traditional teaching about sins which, though objectively grave in respect of matter, are nevertheless subjectively only venial *ex imperfectione actus;* one has only to consider that, according to the teaching of the Church, no exploration, exterior or interior, of a man's acts or attitudes, however detailed, can ever yield an absolute certainty about how that man, in the ultimate depths of his person and his conscience, stands before God; one has only to have heard something, however little, about depth psychology, repression, substitution, self-deception, etc., to have to agree that thousands of "religious" and "moral" acts can take place in man which are induced by training, imitation, suggestion, mere instruction from without and a "good will" which does not reach to the real kernel of the person; acts which are not really religious acts because they do not stem from that level of personality, supernaturally elevated and absolutely individual, whose free fulfilment they must be if they are to signify, before God, the creation of an eternally valid life.

In really religious acts, man does not only fulfil what is most truly his own, his spiritual-personal and grace-endowed individuality; through these acts he also acquires a decisive significance in the salvation of others. We have already said that individuality and universality, when at the same level of being, do not exist in mutually opposed rivalry but are the two sides of one and the same thing, and necessarily increase in the same degree. Now, the Church is the community, founded by the *pneuma* of God, of these personal individuals elevated by supernatural grace. She is not only that. Because she is the supernatural saving community of men in all their dimensions, and because man, even as regards his salvation, is involved in all the complexity of his many-levelled existence, she is also a society of external law, of the spoken word, of the written Scriptures, of the hierarchy, of the gestures of a cult, of the sacraments, of administration and even of bureaucracy. But the Church is necessarily more than all that. And what this "more" means is that the supernatural community of unique, non-interchangeable individuals in interior grace, in the truth and love of Christ, in the self-communication of the three-personed inner life of God, is the most central and the highest of all the many levels of existence in the Church. It is the one which all the others are there to serve, to which they are ordered and from which alone they derive their meaning, their rights and their value, simply in the degree to which they really serve as a medium for the concrete realization of that truly pneumatic community.

Really religious acts (those which do not only seem to be so, but are really done before God as acts of spiritual and grace-endowed individuality) are that by which the life of the Church is constituted and effected in her innermost center and the most intimate reality of her being. So it is where such acts are really taking place that a man becomes of decisive significance in the Church and in the salvation of other men. Of course a man in the Church must do other things as well; or rather, it would be better to say, he must do this essential thing *in* other things: he will receive the sacraments; he will take part in the common, visible worship of God; he will publicly declare his faith; he will read religious literature; he will belong to organizations in the Church; he will in some way support the Church's outward work of missionary extension; he may perhaps belong to a Christian political party; he will work with others at the "Christianization" of social, political and cultural life. And it will no doubt often be precisely in these things and their activities that he will achieve that most real thing, on which everything depends, real religious acts; for all the rest is to a certain degree the embodiment of the personal, grace-given religious life in which he must fulfil himself if he himself is to be real.

True, all these external, tangible things, these things at the pre-personal, pre-pneumatic psychic level, can often have their own importance in themselves as well (money given to the missions by some indifferent person merely because of external suggestive pressure, without any interior participation, is still useful to the missions); but the real thing, which builds up the most central and the highest dimension of the Church, and which is a truly saving event both for the doer himself and for the other members of the Mystical Body of Christ, can never be at this pre-personal, pre-pneumatic level. So, conversely: Whenever anyone, in the innermost depths of his free, responsible conscience, above and beyond all purely external tradition, and against the pressure of "public opinion," truly believes; whenever anyone loves with the innermost power of a heart in which the Spirit of God is poured out, whenever this love is really something more than a biological instinct to protect one's tribe and one's brood (valuable though such instincts, which are created by God, may be); when such love truly loves without reward or advantage or reinsurance, steadfastly; whenever real fidelity to the truth and to the dictates of conscience endures even to death (without being driven to it by the psychic mechanisms of obstinacy, fanaticism or primitive narrow-mindedness); whenever death is accepted in self-surrendering trust as the overmastering approach of the nameless mystery; whenever the courage to be glad is kept alive through all the glooms and depths of depression and the bitterness of life; whenever these and many similar acts of ultimate, radical validity arise from the depths of a spiritual person graced with the *pneuma* of God (and alas, how rare this miracle seems to be in the common life of our days)—then *there* is the true individual, and there is the Church at her most real. And there it is that the individual has real significance for the salvation of others.

For what happens in this way is, in the Body of Christ which is the Church, a direct blessing and grace to others who belong to that same Body of Christ. Christ's acts conveyed salvation: acts which were all integrated into the one act in which he, alone, in an ultimate loneliness and freedom of which we are not capable, out of a depth within his human nature to which we can never completely reach, abandoned his whole being, in love and obedience, to the bottomless abyss which is silence and mystery, and in the act of doing so, called that Incomprehensible by the name of "Father." That single unique act is our redemption; it makes the Church, as the community of those in grace. This most unique of acts, done in the extreme of loneliness, in utter darkness ad emptiness, where no one could follow him, is what constitutes community at its deepest and most all-embracing. Hence the abiding truth: the Church lives by the acts of individuals done within that act by which she is founded.

Because the human acts which we mean can only be done in the grace of God, all such acts derive from that one act. But it is precisely thus that they are participations in the love of God which is creative of individuality, participations in the destiny of Christ, and hence of saving value for others. According to a total, i.e. in a double sense "catholic" understanding,

acts done in the grace of God, validly religious at their very
source, are not only a passive reception of God's grace but are
God's doing in such a way that in them it is really given by God
to men to act, and so to act as really to convey salvation to
others in the Mystical Body of Christ, though the scope and
the manner of it remains hidden within God's governance of
things. And, on the one hand, this effectiveness attaches *only*
to those acts which are truly, validly personal, religious in their
very root; but, on the other hand, it attaches to *all* such acts,
i.e. not only to those which are explicitly directed towards this
end, whether by an interior intention or an outward act.

Hence the truest history of the Church (if only it could be,
or so far as it can be written) would be the history of the
saints. Not only of those who have been canonized, but of all
those in whom there has really taken place this miracle of
pneumatic existence as the discovery of grace-given individuality in a selfless opening of the innermost kernel of the person's being towards God and so towards all spiritual persons.
Everything else in the Church's history may indeed be important and to be valued as the raw material, perhaps necessary
(and indeed indispensable if the act is to be fully valid) for
the fulfilment of this which is most real in her; but in comparison with this most intimate history of the Church it is
secondary, however much may have been written about it on
the pages of ecclesiastical history, and however much it may
have to claim the Church's attention in her capacity as a
society and institution.

III. *Consequences*

If we are right so far, what are the practical pastoral consequences? If we are to answer this question properly, we must
approach it very carefully. It certainly follows from what has
been said, if rightly understood (i.e. if the irreducible plurality
in the dimensions of human nature is taken seriously), that

any absolutely simple monomanic imperative is fundamentally false and contrary to the nature of things. A pastoral approach which recognizes only one recipe for everything, which aims at opening every door with one single key, which thinks itself to be in possession of an Archimedean fulcrum from which it can proceed to move the whole world, is refuted by the simple ontological reflection that man is a plural being; that this plurality, despite the fact that man is also a unity, is something that a man himself cannot get beyond; and that (if the existential significance of this plurality is not to be, in practice, denied) there can be no one single point for him from which everything can be surveyed, everything worked out and everything directed. Neither pope nor emperor nor any principle, however materially complete and practicable, can claim a totalitarian control over everything. The humility and patience which goes with plurality, with a multiplicity of forces and methods, with God alone as the one irreplaceable point in which they all coincide, belongs to the creaturely humility to be found in truly Christian pastoral work.

But from this it follows, again, that to recommend some one method, to emphasize the attention due to this or that factor, to strive to make clear some particular discovery and to recommend its application in practice, must not be regarded, automatically, as an attack on, a denigration or rejection of, other methods, other efforts and other insights. When we are speaking "catholicly," any particular pronouncement is always to be understood within a larger and more all-embracing context, even when this is not explicitly stated; for one cannot always say everything at once. If a man can bear to hear only what he would say himself, if he regards as an opponent anyone who says anything unexpected or anything which does not actually support his own position, then his attitude is intolerant and uncatholic. It is not always possible to say everything at once. But we should try to hear every individual thing within the broad, free context of all that is

to be understood along with it. Pronouncements all bearing
in *one* direction can never afford to forget ontological plural-
ism, and its consequences, either in the making or the hearing
of them.

Despite this necessary absence of "one-track" principles in
pastoral practice, it is nevertheless possible to deduce a few
basic propositions from what has been said above about the
individual and his significance to the Church in regard to
salvation; and it may be useful to examine them, for two
reasons. In the first place, what we have been saying leads to
pastoral principles of permanent validity, because the individual's reality and significance to salvation exist always and
in every age; and these principles, as regards their timeless
validity, do not particularly need any further development.
But on the other hand, these maxims, deducible from what we
have been saying, do have a particularly immediate significance and urgency today. Even what is always ontologically
valid has a history in regard to the explicit recognition of it,
and in regard to the urgency, the difficulty and the individual
manner of carrying it out. Hence it may well be possible to say
that now, today, is the hour of pneumatic individuality and its
importance to the Church. For on the one hand we are in-
disputably living in an age (the age of vast populations,
psychological techniques of mass-influence, increased depend-
ence of everyone on everyone else, etc.) which involves special
risks to the spiritual, and hence also the pneumatic, individuality of each person. And on the other hand one might at least
raise the question whether the Church, as she proceeds on her
way through history towards her consummation in the Lord's
parousia, is not bound to become more and more aware of her
own nature as the community of pneumatic individuals, and to
have to express this nature in more and more concrete terms
in her life.

For while it is true that the Church is always conscious of
her own nature, yet just as there is a development of dogma,

there is a development, an unfolding, a deepening in that part of the Church's insight into the faith which is constituted by her self-consciousness of her own nature. And hence it is by no means impossible that the Church is becoming more clearly and radically conscious than in earlier days of her nature as a pneumatic community of unique individuals: more conscious both in explicit theory and (which is more difficult and more important) in pastoral practice. Secular human development points, indeed, in the same direction. For while it is indeed true that we live in an age of mass-humanity, of vast states with almost omnipotent power to influence the most intimate levels of individual life, yet it is also true that the historical development which has produced these phenomena is a development which does at least make possible an intensive individual life for the maximum number of people. And why should not the Church, in her theory and practice, become the champion of *this* particular meaning of modern history? It does then make sense to ask why and in what direction these permanently valid principles concerning the pneumatic individual, his status in himself and his significance to the Church, have a specially urgent relevance today. We cannot of course hope to draw all the possible conclusions, nor even to maintain that those we do draw are really the most important.

The first thing of which we must speak is the necessity of having the courage, in pastoral work, to think in terms of the individual. Of course there can be no question of the Church's really giving up, from her side, fundamentally, her wish to be a people's Church, the Church of the masses. Whether she will in fact go on being such a thing in the future, God alone knows. But it is certain that she always has the task and the obligation of striving to be, to remain and to become such a Church. For while it is true that God reserves to himself alone the ultimate concern for the fulfilment of his general will for salvation, and can achieve it even where the Church achieves nothing, yet the Church has no right to make any fundamental

exclusion of any particular human beings from her concern
and her missionary responsibility, and to settle down to being
fundamentally a "sect" in the theological sense or an esoteric
circle of a few elect.

But even without going into the obscure and difficult question of how far permanently valid principles do justifiably vary
in their stringency and binding force at any particular time,
in the degree of intensity with which they really require us to
strive for their realization; without asking ourselves how far
the Church is required to exert herself at this present time
with the object of retaining her position in public life, or
whether she may perhaps be in a position to realize that,
without prejudice to her desire to maintain this characteristic
of her nature, she does not need, according to the will of
God, to throw herself totally in this particular direction—
without going into these questions, we can in any case say
that to think in terms of the individual is an especially necessary virtue in pastoral work today. It does not mean that we
are calling anything else sour grapes, nor that we are making
a virtue of necessity; what we are doing is having that virtue
without which the real nature of the Church would suffer even
if the mass Church of public life were not in such evident
straits. For it is only when Christianity has really reached the
individual in his own unique individuality that there has been
any decisive success in the pastoral field, and this not only in
that individual's salvation but in the conferring of blessing on
the Church. But it is by no means a foregone conclusion that
these real, decisive successes will be particularly numerous
when the mass Church, as such, is flourishing and operating
without let or hindrance. It is perfectly thinkable that the great
mass of people should be willing to be marshalled as a united
body, to be shaped alike by the same moral code, to hold and
to practice the same "conviction," and yet that the real thing
which all this is supposed to mean and to aim at should be
wanting or only very sparsely present.

Who, for instance, would be so bold as to maintain that in the Middle Ages a higher percentage of the population was living in the grace of God than is the case today? Nobody could seriously maintain or prove either this or the opposite statement, though it is beyond question that, sociologically speaking, a more homogeneous kind of "Christendom" existed in the Middle Ages, or even in nineteenth-century bourgeois society, than does today. But if you do not dare to conclude, from the indubitable fact of a greater degree of homogeneous "Christendom" at an earlier period, that there were then relatively more Christians in the grace of God than there are today, you must in fact admit that the achievement of the widest and most homogeneous measure possible of Christianity in the empirical sphere of social and institutional life, in normal morality, public opinion, tradition and custom (desirable though all this may be) is no guarantee that there will be any large number of real Christians in God's sight. Fundamentally these still always have to be specially created even where a homogeneously Christian milieu is already in existence. The faith which changes hearts, the love of God which truly justifies, are just as much an unimaginable, unique miracle of God's grace when they take place in the environment of a Church which embraces the mass of the population; a miracle which, even in so far as it is sustained also by human causes, depends to a very large extent on causes other than those operating in a mass-population Church.

In this too it is like love. Plenty of marriages take place, and one can hope that plenty of marriages are true communions of love; but every real love is a unique and completely new miracle, which is not made commonplace by the fact that it often happens, nor does it depend simply on those causes which may lead to marriage even where no such living love is present. Hence the desire that there shall be such individuals is not simply a part of the desire for a mass Church, and its object and goal is not to contribute to the strengthening and establishment of the Church's general sociological influence in the pre-personal dimension, using pre-personal means.

If the individual only exists as a Christian and the genuine, real Christian only as an individual (impossible and impermissible though it is for the individual Christian to exist in isolation on his own), then there must be a pastoral approach to the individual and the mentality for such an approach; and at the root of this mentality must lie the conviction that a human act which is truly personal and supernatural in its ultimate depths is a greater event than a thousand acts which only outwardly seem to be such. To give a crude comparison: a form of propaganda which addresses itself only to man's pre-personal level and to mere mechanisms of association, or, indeed, techniques which directly affect only his unconscious, can, say, achieve the result that one thousand people do their washing with Persil. At the same time one might perhaps convince one person on factual grounds that it actually is the right washing-powder to use, being better than any other. In this matter the only ultimately important thing, of course, is to get the washing done with the right stuff. Hence (assuming that this *is* the best stuff) the best thing to do is to use the first form of propaganda. But if what the propaganda (of either kind) is aiming at is precisely the act of personal conviction, then it may indeed make use of these pre-personal techniques, because personal conviction may in certain circumstances be facilitated by them, though it may be endangered as well; but such propaganda cannot claim to have attained its goal if what it is aiming at is merely performed in an external way, without its being established at the same time that the performance springs from that personal conviction without which it would not be what was being aimed at at all. In such a case, the employment of all these pre-personal propaganda techniques, even if we assume them to be successful, will leave the really important and decisive thing still to do.

Our pastoral work is and must to a great extent be a pre-personal approach, influencing children, training adolescents, influencing public opinion, maintaining moral standards and customs, etc. A great deal, even, in our missionary pastoral work which is, considered in itself, addressed to the spiritual person, to his spiritual judgment and moral responsibility, will often in fact, even while achieving a success, be arrested in this pre-personal dimension of human life. But we must see, and we must keep telling ourselves, that all *this* pastoral work, even when successful, is not the ultimate and real point of pastoral work. True, it will often happen that, starting as an impulse in the pre-personal dimension, it will transplant itself into the deeper, personal heart of a man, so that at the right moment, under the grace of God, by a sort of *generatio aequivoca*, something will arise there which is greater and higher than anything that that impulse could have effected in itself. But even so it remains true that the pastoral effort must have the will to awaken this truly personal, grace-given, unique thing in the depths of the man, and must not console itself with the thought that this can, in the end, only be awakened by the grace of God.

From this we see that we need to have, far more than perhaps we do have, the charismatic pastor; the man to whom Nicodemus can come in the night as he came to Jesus; the man in whose truly authentic religious existence even the sceptical man of today can believe, without getting the impression that it is a secondary, not personally authentic, product of tradition, a result of being entangled in the clerical office. Are we not often lacking in such pastors, men who are capable of being "prototypes" of real religious existence in all its authenticity? Are there enough pastors who radiate the power to awaken others? How many priests are there who are brave enough to pray aloud, spontaneously; to speak of the more sublime things in the spiritual life; uninhibited enough to say anything spiritual, outside the discharge of their office, in a fully personal way? Do we not get the impression, here and there, that re-

course is had to official, organizational, sodality-type procedures because we dare not lay claim to any experience or
success at the most important and most sublime level of real
pastoral work? It is true that there is a highly suspect thing
described as individual pastoral care, rightly mistrusted by
many real pastors; but it is not really any such thing, because
while its dealings are with the individual (in monastic parlors
and personal contacts, etc.), they are not at that level at which
a man in his inmost heart decides for God. But the fact that an
"individual apostolate" of this sort (corresponding to a craving
for contact in the pastor himself and the soul concerned rather
than to the dispensing of salvation) is often used as an alibi to
excuse one from working in the mass apostolate does not mean
that the latter, either, can be regarded as the only one or the
only important one. There must be truly individual pastoral
work and the courage to think in terms of the individual. It
is here, after all, that God's decisive battles are fought.

And there is this to be considered: a homogeneous environment, a general standard of morality and public opinion, the
practice of the mass of people, etc., are all subject to a rather
odd law: their influence on the individual's intimate personal
attitude does not always increase in direct proportion to their
own growth. When something is simply taken for granted in a
general way as an indisputable law by everybody, it no longer
confronts the individual as a demand for his personal decision;
for many of the masses it is no longer something that they
personally realize at all. There is probably an optimum level
(itself varying according to place and period) of maximum
capacity for personal realization of Christianity, and this precisely *not* in a maximally "Christian" environment. Just as in a
cuboid, a larger surface area does not automatically imply a
larger volume, so the maximum public recognition of Christianity does not necessarily imply the maximum concrete possibility for an existential appropriation of Christianity by a
large number of individuals.

This may perhaps give us a clue to why God has willed that Christianity and the Church should always have been combated and never become self-evident, indisputable factors in history and public life. If they did become so, they would in practice be interiorly and personally accepted by fewer people than is the case when opposition to Christianity makes it possible and necessary to take a personal decision. This alone would demonstrate the fundamental falsity of changing the milieu, though this is not, of course, an argument against having this kind of apostolate as well.

Christians are essentially and always individuals, even when there are many such individuals, and even if everybody were such an individual. And because it is so, we must think in terms of the individual and of pastoral work directed to the individual as such. And suppose we had an age in which there were few explicit Christians and many non-Christians, with the Church claiming few people and the others many, and if one nevertheless could (and had to) hope that among these non-Christians claimed by the others the greater number were saved by God, one would then have to say: The many whom the other side have, they have not as real individuals, but only on those pre-personal human dimensions in which a man is not really himself. But then it might always be true that the Church has more people than the other side; while one man praying in the loneliness of his own conscience would always be more than a thousand marching behind a red banner. Why then should we not have the courage to think in terms of the individual in our pastoral work?

The second thing that can be deduced as a sort of guiding rule from our theoretical considerations is the principle that the Christian life must be known and lived as real living, and not as a mere fulfilment of norms and observation of commandments. What this means is something that could also be deduced from other approaches. But it is particularly easy to understand it on the principles developed here. For if a

Christian life is always the fulfilment of unique pneumatic individuality, it is self-evident that it cannot consist only in fulfilling and respecting such norms, general laws and commandments as come from outside a man. Of course there is God's holy will, confronting man as an unconditional "Thou shalt." Of course this divine will is also made known to man through the law as proclaimed to him. But according to the teaching of the Scriptures this law ceases to be the mere sting of sin (though holy in itself) only when it is more than a norm, only when it works from within as the power of the Holy Spirit, as an interior, God-given inclination; it is God who gives by grace that which he commands, and this grace is the most intimately interior thing that there is in us; and further, the universal law (which we do have and which is valid) is only really fulfilled when each of us grasps how to carry it out in the way which is required of *us,* a way made concrete and unique in and with the uniqueness of the individual and his personal divine vocation. If all this is so, then we can understand that the individual's Christianity can and must be experienced no less, to say the least, as an intimate vitality pressing outwards from within to inform the rest of life than as a norm confronting us from outside with its demand of "Thou shalt" and its claim on our respect.

It is precisely when we are approaching the individual as such that we need to be aware of this. For the very thing that he does not want is to be treated as an object with purely objective norms. He wants to find himself. He wants an answer to the questions which oppress him from within. He wants to be freed from his own inner bondage. He wants to become what he is. None of this represents any new truth. We have always preached that the commandments of God are in their true sense a liberation and protection, not a narrowing, constricting compulsion. But this is something that does not only need to be said in general but to become a reality that can be experienced individually by the individual.

Christianity has to grow from its own principle of life. Of course it also has to be transmitted to men from outside. But it would be a false understanding of what preaching is, whether by the authoritative *magisterium* or the pastor in his official work, to suppose that it can or should transmit Christianity to a man as though he were, at best, an empty hollow space ready and waiting for it, or a schoolboy hearing of Australia for the first time in a geography lesson. The grace of God has always been there ahead of our preaching; a man is always in a true sense a Christian already when we begin to commend Christianity to him. For he is a man, already included in God's general will for salvation, redeemed by Christ, with grace already living and working in his innermost heart at least as the proffered possibility of supernatural action. Hence our preaching is not really an indoctrination with something alien from outside but the awakening of something within, as yet not understood but nevertheless really present; something that is not, of course, to be misunderstood in the modernist sense as a natural religious need in the human subconscious, but which is a grace of God.

Any approach to a man in words from outside, if it is Christian, is always an appeal to God who is already speaking by grace within him and being in some sense heard; any communication of Christianity is always a communication of what is already there, alive, within a man. And if it often seems to be otherwise: if people get the impression that we are preaching a very extraordinary, remote doctrine, intelligible only to experts, which no normal man could find interesting unless he stopped being an ordinary man, it is not because Christianity is really like this but because we have not rightly understood it. We have only half grasped it, and instead of the other, equally necessary, half we fall back on the power of tradition, which still, perhaps, works effectively for us, so that we think it is bound to be just as convincing for everybody else and are highly astonished when this is not so.

Of course Christianity proclaims mysteries, absolute mysteries, which are made known only by God's revelation and still remain mysteries to the human intellect even after they have been proclaimed. But this statement does not mean that the mysteries can be transmitted to men only from outside. They too, indeed precisely they, are spoken by God from within. For it is precisely because there are mysteries in Christianity, precisely because they can be meaningfully assimilated only by a divinely elevated understanding, that the grace of faith, of the supernatural light of faith, is necessary; and because this exists, it is precisely mystery that is preached from within by God.

Further: this Christianity already present as a life within a man, to which we must appeal if the individual as such is to be reached, is not only given by this most inward grace regarded in itself as something completely abstract. Life, as such, in the concrete, everyday life, has an inward openness towards God through that grace which is constantly being offered to it, grace which desires to become living and fruitful in the very concreteness of this life. Joy, seriousness, responsibility, daring, commitment to an unforeseeable future, love, birth, the burden of work and thousands of other aspects of life which everyone experiences have an undercurrent which comes from grace and leads into it, if they are rightly interpreted and really accepted in their true, undiluted being. It is on this presupposition that we can hope that there are many who are Christians without explicitly knowing it, that grace is more widely accepted than is recorded in the Church's statistics of reception of the sacraments and other explicitly grace-bearing historical events. These events in human life relate to Christianity in the first place because they cannot be even truly human, fully and in the long run, except by the grace of Christ; and hence, when they are so, they bear mute witness to the grace of God in Christ, they are victories of God's saving will, who creates salvation through his interior grace.

But beyond this, because they exist in a concrete order which is called to the supernatural, they are not in fact, even in their own concrete nature, simply "natural." Their permanent naturalness is, in the concrete, always open, pointing beyond itself, not indeed because of anything in their nature in the abstract but because they are part of this concrete order of things in which they are willed by God *as* factors in a supernatural order. The relationship to the God of that supernatural order, their state of being subject to his inescapable claim upon them, really determines what they are (even though it is a determination only conferred by grace); it is a permanent and continuous determination, not a mere juridical concept.

For example, death as man in fact experiences it is not death as it might be experienced in a purely natural order of things. It is the death of a man who, because of the claim of grace upon him (grace whose total essence is consummated only when it overcomes and excludes death), experiences and suffers death as something *wrong* (even if only unthinkingly and inexplicitly) to a quite different degree from a man undergoing death in an order without grace, without Christ's resurrection, in which disembodiment would be an obvious, completely normal event required by the whole concrete order of things. Love between persons takes on an absolute quality, a depth unattainable in a purely natural order, in so far as it is an inescapable fact experienced (whether consciously or not) as a factor within a love (whether awaiting consummation or already consummated) whose root is the love of the Holy Ghost for the Father. When in the concrete order of reality someone has the experience of utter loneliness, accepts it, does not run away from it, lets it have its way, then this spiritual experience, in which God is present (present in the silent emptiness where there is no apparent comfort, no reassurance to which one might cling), is, at least to one who believes as a Christian, not only a natural spiritual experience but an experience of the grace of God, in which a real unique Christianity becomes itself.

Probably many more, and more intelligible, examples of grace experienced in everyday life would need to be pointed out and interpreted. We cannot do this here. But perhaps this is enough to convey a little of what is meant by saying that human life does of itself present a kind of anonymous Christianity, which explicit Christianity can then interpret, giving a man the courage to accept and not run away from what he experiences and undergoes in his own life; to take hold on it as the gracious miracle of God's love. It is where Christian preaching sets out to encounter the individual that we should apply this pneumatic "depth psychology" (quite different in kind, of course, from what is usually so described). This would be putting into practice what Saint Paul said of his preaching: "What therefore you worship [really worship!] without knowing it [as consciously and explicitly interpreted], that I preach to you" (Acts 17, 23). It is obvious that this guidance of a Christian towards finding himself, towards assimilating the Christianity which comes to us "by hearing" (Rom. 10, 17) through the discovery of its grace-given inwardness (already imparted in the underlying meaning of everything we experience in this redeemed world) is the essential, if not actually the exclusive, concern of individual pastoral work. It is only when a man can thus be brought face to face with the individual concreteness of his own life that he can fully grasp the Christian quality of that life, which is something he cannot produce himself but must accept as already given by God.

From this standpoint we can indicate, too, a sublime apostolate for the lay Christian. This unlocking of the Christian meaning, as yet not understood, in the events of an individual life is not essentially bound up with holding an ecclesiastical office: so far, indeed, as anyone can be helped by someone else in this matter at all. Such help depends chiefly on having experienced this kind of understanding in one's own life, on being able to be, in attitude more than in word, a prototype for this conscious acceptance of one's life in all its hidden christened-ness. It is indeed a priest's duty, so as to give his official apostolate its maximum possibility of fruitfulness, to apply himself to being as "spiritual" a man as possible, with experience of these mysterious questions which are posed by real life. But there is nothing in the nature of the case to make this a privilege of the clergy. Indeed, it will often happen that those who are not "experts" know more about this maieutic drawing forth of individual Christianity. The witness of an individual life is often the best, indeed the only possible, initiation into the mystery that in becoming a Christian one is simply finding oneself in one's own ultimate truth as a grace given by God. And only those who do thus find Christianity, who thus discover an ultimate identity between themselves and official Christianity, are "individual" Christians: but this is what everyone must be, because he who is a Christian only because that is what "one" is, is not really one at all.

A lot could be said in this section. For we have so far done little more than state a very abstract principle. How much would need to be said to fill in the content of this principle? We should have to speak (to give just a few arbitrary examples) of the process of arriving, by direction and practice, at a truly personal prayer; of choice (of a particular profession, marriage, etc.) as a religious precipitate, and in general of discovering the concrete will of God; of a truly personal use of the sacrament of penance, and of overcoming the legalistic and magical notions that obscure the understanding and performance of the sacraments in general; of loneliness and inactivity as Christian attitudes, of a Christian performance of such everyday things as sleeping, eating and similar primary themes of life. All this and much besides ought not to be seen as some sublime extra, added to real life for "those who can afford it," but as perfectly simple, basically obvious (and *therefore* mysterious) modes of life which arise of themselves out of any genuinely individual life, i.e. one which has come to itself. And in this way a man could gradually come to understand that he would be surrendering his very self if he chose not to be a Christian. And it is only if he has got as far as this that he is a Christian capable of being one as an individual.

A third thing to be said is this: If the individual has this indispensable significance for salvation, then room must be provided in the Church for this individual Christianity. It is not, of course, a question of the Church's ever in principle refusing room to a Christian for individual, free discovery of himself. Today, moreover, the Church does not dispose of any power that she could use to try to force those acts which, by their very nature, must be free acts. But there is, historically, a variation of more and less in the room allotted by the Church to this individual self-discovery by Christians; freedom is sometimes more, sometimes less, valued. Do we not sometimes find ourselves thinking that one starts being a "good Catholic" at the point where one starts being "organized," even over and above the ordinary life of the Church? I would not for the world say anything against the necessity and beneficence of sodalities, organizations and (often highly organized) "movements." They are not only a sensible and often necessary continuation and articulation of the Church's own social nature; today, of all times, when the individual on his own is powerless against the many, they are indispensable. But it is possible to ask ourselves whether, necessary as all this is, the even more necessary thing is not often forgotten, or not kept vividly in mind: namely, that all this is only useful and meaningful in so far as it directly or indirectly makes it possible to be a Christian standing before God as an individual.

Perhaps a good deal of the organized activity in the Church during the nineteenth century was based on the tacit assumption that the whole of "secular" life (except for what was merely economic and technical) could and should be kept within the Church's sphere by means of religious-cultural organizations. Thus one starts by wanting (rightly) to have a Catholic school where, in an explicitly religious environment, the riches of education and culture can be offered to the growing child so that he can experience the synthesis between culture and Christianity in the most living and palpable way possible and so learn to achieve it in his own life; and one then goes on, in the same way, to try to extend the same attempt, through Church organizations, to the whole of life as lived by Christians. The aim was a sort of cultural autonomy, and this (leaving aside the justifications arising from ecclesiastical politics and the protection of the Church and Christianity in public life) called for a multitude of Church organizations. But is there not a concealed mistake here? Have we taken enough account of the fact that in this age an ecclesiastical cultural autarchy of this sort is simply not possible any more? That even if everyone were a good Christian it would not really be possible, because the sphere of the secular and profane has simply got too large and too differentiated and too explicitly constituted in its own (relative) autonomy for it all to be included in any ecclesiastical framework, however loosely-knit?

But if it is not possible, if the individual Christian simply cannot live his life exclusively in a context of explicitly ecclesiastical character (reading Catholic newspapers, belonging to Catholic trade and professional unions, going in for sport in Catholic sports clubs and fulfilling his social needs in Catholic societies), must he not then learn to be a Christian on his own, and must he not then be recognized as a good Christian and allowed to think of himself as such while demanding a certain amount of space in his life, free from Church organizations, in which he can set about becoming and being an individual Christian? And is it not necessary for the Church's organizations all to practice an "open door" policy, such as will give "outsiders" the feeling that it is possible to go into them without thereby declaring that one absolutely and permanently belongs there? In other words, should not our organizations be

occasions for constant fresh encounters between an irreversibly
secularized culture, no longer directly subject to the Church's
influence, on the one hand, and Christianity and the Church
on the other; rather than attempts at ecclesiastical cultural
autarchy? And this, if for no other reason, because it is becoming plainer and plainer that there is simply no such thing,
in the concrete, as an obligatory Christian culture (a Christian
constitution of the state; an economic program clearly deduced
from Christian principles; art which, being Christian in inspira-
tion, has the right to be admired by all good Christians, etc.).

There are still further occasions for remembering that we
shall only have the kind of Christians that we need to have if
they are Christians as individuals, and that they must be given
room to make this possible. For example, there are indeed
those ecclesiastical nonconformists who go in for grousing,
contradiction and protest for mere reasons of make-up and
temperament; who think something false for no better reason
than that it is the opinion of the majority or of ecclesiastical
authority, but are highly conformist among themselves. But
does not the opposite fault exist as well? Too little understanding, among the Church's leaders, her clergy, and the broad
mass of her people, that it is possible for Christians to hold an
opinion differing from that of the rest, which it can also be
permissible to express; that Christians who live their religious
life in a way of their own are not thereby necessarily "uncatholic"; that *sentire cum Ecclesia* does not necessarily and
always involve thinking that everything that happens at the
official or administrative or clerical level is good and splendid?
Of course every reasonable person in the Church does in principle admit that there not only are in practice but *ought* to be
differences of opinion and manner of life among Catholic
Christians. But is this recognition in principle sufficiently
carried out in practice, seeing that it is only where there is an
area of freedom that individuals can become Christians and
Christians can become individuals? Do we see clearly enough,

in regard to that venerable maxim *in necessariis unitas, in dubiis libertas,* that unity in essentials, if it is to be what it must be (a unity of many individuals in a personal, responsible conviction), is possible in the long run only if *in dubiis libertas* is really taken seriously, not treated as a mere secondary concession but as a necessary condition for the first part of the maxim?

Are we really allowing the formation of that public opinion in the Church which Pius XII declared was an unconditional necessity for her? Is it clear to everybody that if such a thing is to be formed, the Church, even in her public life, is going to have to be tolerant and patient in letting individuals speak out, even if the immediate effect is that the chorus of voices is no longer harmonious? Or are we always scared that any difference of opinion in the life of the Church is automatically a sign of weakness and damaging "disunity"? Or, again, are we always afraid of "giving scandal" by letting people see (as the "others" have known for a long time, anyway) that even the Church does not have a ready-made store of the best prescriptions for all concrete problems, and that therefore we have to argue with each other and thus slowly reach agreement, not just *any* agreement but as good a practical decision as we can manage?

Let us draw one fourth and final consequence of our fundamental considerations. Individuality and community are not really competing opposites between which we have to choose. But there is indeed (as we said) a certain relative opposition between individuality at one level of reality (both as a whole and within a person) and universality at some other level. And in this respect we can certainly look for intermediate links that may serve to bind together the two halves of a relative opposition of this sort, to the extent that it needs to be overcome. So we can ask ourselves what concrete intermediary there might conceivably be between individuality at the personal and pneumatic level, on the one hand, and universality at the social and

organizational level on the other, the latter belonging ontologically (in the whole order of humanity and the Church) to
a lower level. When we ask this we are looking for something
that will, on the one hand, give the greatest possible scope to
what is really spiritual, personal, pneumatic, something that
will be as directly as possible sustained by it, and yet something, on the other hand, that will signify a certain social
solidarity.

This mediating link need not have the character of a hybrid,
for the simple reason that the conflict in which it is to mediate,
because it exists within the unity of man and the Church, is
essentially a relative one, an opposition in unity, and hence
really reconcilable and resolvable (though having due regard
to the permanent plurality of this unity). It is possible to
designate this mediating link with a name already in current
use, and thus, conversely, to determine the real character of
what we are designating. The link we are looking for is called
the "cell." It is not possible to get at the sociological nature of
what we mean if the word is understood, in this connection,
in purely organizational or biological terms. The peculiar character of the "cell," as a social and pastoral concept in the
Church, must rather be understood from the point of view that
we have here indicated. The "cell" is a way for men to come
together in the social dimension, and is nevertheless still based
on the special individual character of each member, on his own
direct power to draw men and to be a prototype. Hence it is a
small group; it aims to give the individual room, to work in a
"man to man" fashion; it has to accept and take into account
a certain instability of structure arising out of its very nature;
its numbers can increase only slowly; it cannot be "drilled"
and organized bureaucratically from above.

One might perhaps outline too, from this viewpoint, the difference between a Christian "cell" of this kind and a Communist one. The Communist cell is merely the smallest unit in a
huge communal organization which reduces all to a dead level

and does not recognize any uniquely irreplaceable individuality; it is a function of a totalitarian conception of man and society. A cell in the Christian understanding of it, existing for the mission and apostolate of the Church, is a coming together in community in which the individual and his unique importance in the scheme of salvation are most directly asserted and brought into action. But the pastoral theology of the significance and task of the cell in the Church will have to be dealt with elsewhere.

4

MARY AND THE APOSTOLATE

We are here to take counsel together in serious matters. Our purpose is to arrive by general discussion at norms for pastoral practice; norms which, even though they are "the letter," will not extinguish the spirit; which, while leaving the spirit supreme, will force us to distinguish between the spirit and vague, undisciplined enthusiasms; and which will guard against anyone's continuing to do nothing at all or to let things carry on as before, on the pretext that things cannot be entirely regulated from above, by decisions taken at conference tables. The ultimate problem in any attempt of this kind is, fundamentally, the problem of Christianity itself: for Christianity is at once the religion of the Spirit and the religion of the Word made flesh. Hence it is the religion of which we can say that where the Spirit is, there is freedom; here the letter of the law is overcome; here the Spirit breathes where he will; we are no longer in servitude to men; our instruction is by our anointing; and there is to be no binding of fresh burdens on top of those which the fathers were unable to bear.

But this same Christianity is the religion of him who became man, and hence of the visible Church, of the legally constituted Church, of the tangible sacraments, of the holding of office, of the fullness of power, of humility; the religion which does not shrink from continuing and fulfilling the descent of God into the flesh of this world and which does not regard everything

concrete, clear-cut, commanded, institutional, social and traditional as automatically unspiritual and anti-Christian. Christianity is the religion of that Spirit which comes in the blood
of him who became man and died in obedience upon the cross;
it is the religion of the tangible indissolubly wedded to the
Spirit. The unity is a permanent miracle of God's grace; it is
the ever-recurring, ever newly-performed miracle of unity between heaven and earth, law and liberty, grace and justice,
flesh and spirit. And if we find that we too are always having
to strive again for this unity—even at such a conference as
this—to pray for it, suffer for it, sacrifice for it, rethink it and
reapply it; if this is something that is always having to happen
afresh, there is nothing here to wonder at, no cause for scandal.
For a true Christian and a true priest, this is something entirely
obvious. He will not despise norms merely because they are no
substitute for the Spirit; nor will he idolize them, for they do
not constitute any absolute guarantee that the Spirit always
breathes wherever they are respected.

1. The Need to Consider the Nature and the New Tasks of the Church

If we are seeking, not indeed to settle the question of the
concrete norms for pastoral work, Catholic Action, and the
apostolates of the clergy and laity but to clarify our minds on
the basic principles which the right answers will in each case
have to involve, we find ourselves impelled to turn our eyes
towards Mary. Not merely because there is a sense in which
we have still to celebrate the conclusion of the Marian Year,
to gather in its harvest in the field of pastoral theology. There
is a deeper reason: every fresh consideration of pastoral questions, every new initiative in the field, must issue, ultimately,
from a deepened understanding of that which is at once the
medium and the goal of all pastoral work, namely the Church.

It is not a matter of chance that in this age of world wars,

world revolutions, the close of what has been the modern age
and the beginning of the atomic age, and the uniting together
of what have been till now the histories of separate peoples
into a single, world-wide history of mankind, the theology of
the Church has become a favorite theme among theologians
and in the religious thought of the faithful. For in a new age
of this kind, which is changing probably far more, not less,
profoundly than we think, the Church which is in such a
world must also, of necessity, be entering upon a new epoch,
no matter what the Church's prospects in the new age are
going to be. This being the case, the Church has got to give
thought both to her own nature and to her task in this new
age. She must do both: for it is not this age, itself blind and
imperilled, which can tell her what she has to do, but only
her own nature and her own mandate, eternally ancient and
ever new. But reflection on her own nature, in all its fullness
and splendor, will not yield any imperative course of concrete
action in the pastoral field unless we confront such reflection,
boldly and uninhibitedly, with the special character of the new
age; unless, then, we have the courage to consider what are
the Church's new tasks, and do not turn the theology of the
Church into a romantic escape from the crying needs and the
special blessings of this age into a cloud cuckoo-land of abstract theology.

II. Mary—Type of the Church

But if we are to think about the nature of the Church—and
the Church, moreover, as boldly laying herself bare to the real
actualities of a given historical situation as a demand made
upon her and a burden laid upon her—it will be well to look
at Mary. For in her as a concrete person, in her acts and in
her destiny, we can see more clearly what the Church actually
is than in purely abstract concepts. As St. Ambrose said,
Maria typus Ecclesiae. It is not only that Mariology can

profit from Ecclesiology; that a broad, full-scale theology of the Church, from within which Mary can be assigned her place in the being and functioning of that Church, can be of great service to Mariology and safeguard it against sentimental distortions and subjectivist isolation. The reverse possibility has just as much meaning: Mariology fertilizes Ecclesiology. The Church is not a substance; she is a happening, an event, constantly renewed in concrete human beings. So it is at these that we must look if we want to know what the Church is. But considered as a redeemed human being, a fruit of the redemption (and this is the dimension in which the Church moves) there is no one who could more clearly represent what Christian existence is than the most blessed Virgin Mother of God. And because we know of her by faith from the start, even independently of a developed theology of the Church, we know of the Church because and in so far as we know of her. Thus there is a path from Mariology to Ecclesiology, because, as we might also say, there is a path from Christology to Ecclesiology, and Christology, considered in its concrete content, as it actually is in saving history, *is* Mariology as well; simply because the Word of God in the flesh is from the Virgin, and this very taking of flesh is, immediately and really, saving history; which, as such, took place in the faith and in the womb of Mary, so that we confess in the creed: born of the Virgin Mary.

III. Mary—Type of the Apostolate and of Pastoral Work

We cannot undertake to give here even the barest sketch of a complete ecclesiology such as must result if its point of conception is a true, i.e. Christological, Mariology. It would take us much too far afield. We mean to consider Mary simply in so far as she is a type of the apostolate and of the pastoral work of the Church. But we will just indicate, in a few preliminary remarks, that a theme of this kind does not belong merely to the department of pious "accommodated senses" and far-fetched comparisons and parallels, but has its real place in the actual subject-matter of faith and theology.

1. *Mary: the Supreme Instance of Redemption in Its Coming and Its Acceptance*

We shall have, from the start, a stunted view of the essence and significance of the blessed Virgin if we take as our point of departure a merely biological motherhood in her. According to the witness of Scripture she is by faith, through her personal assent, the mother of the eternal Word. Hence it is not merely that by a purely biological process she gives a human nature to the person of the Logos (though even by this alone she would be Mother of God in the sense declared at Ephesus). Rather, she is the Mother of God through a decision of faith: through an event which is itself, as such, a part of saving history, and of saving history in its full, public, official sense. This is because the object and goal of this event is the incarnation of the divine Word, i.e. the very heart and center of saving history; and because in this event of becoming man redemption is already pre-defined, though it remains to be worked out on the cross.

For the coming of the Logos in the flesh of sin is already the decisive act of redemption, a redemption which then unfolds, inevitably, from that event; it is not simply the constituting of a divine-human Person who then, merely as a matter of fact, went on to achieve the redemption, as a sort of additional decision and subsequent destiny. From this it follows that Mary stands at the decisive point in saving history as she who receives into herself the salvation of the world in an act which is at once official and personal. Her co-operation (as an act of hers) is the act of receiving, of acceptance, not of primary initiative; it is an act which itself is performed by the power of redemption coming upon her and itself creating her acceptance of it. But this is how she is decisive in the salvation of the world. If—corresponding to the eschatological structure of salvation, historically visible and final, not subject to cancellation, and hence, as historical and final, possessing an ultimately indissoluble and indestructible unity of history and grace, office and person, official mission and charism, sign and signified—if, corresponding to all this, we have in Mary an absolute correspondence between the office and the personal accomplishment of the mission involved in it (and it is precisely this to which Scripture testifies), then what we have in Mary is simply the supreme instance of redemption as coming and accepted. Mary is she who is perfectly redeemed. Because this is what she is, everything comes together in her: her own grace, and the salvation of others; the receiving of salvation according to Spirit and faith, and the acceptance of it according to the flesh; official service and personal charism; pure passivity and spontaneous act; action, and submission to being acted upon—all reach at once their highest fulfilment and their complementary unity.

If the Church is simply the historical, visible unity, in grace, of the redeemed, by acceptance of Christ in flesh and in spirit, then Mary is of necessity the supreme instance of that event which is the Church, she is the type of the Church as such. Hence what the Church is, in her functioning, is shown at its clearest and in its pure, full completeness in the Mary-event. This is the supreme case of active and passive redemption, seen in absolute purity and luminous uniqueness; the supreme case, then, of that event in which a human being, endowed with grace, accepts grace in and through that grace, both for himself and for others, so that the acceptance which is personal for himself implies salvation for others, and the acceptance which is a co-operation in the salvation of others is precisely that act in which the grace of God is accepted for himself; in

which the service which is one's office and one's own sanctification becomes simply one and the same.

2. *Mary: the Living Pattern of the Apostolate*

But from this it follows that Mary and her work are the
supreme and wholly typical case of the apostolate of a human
being, in so far as he is distinct from Jesus Christ, the Mediator
of salvation. It is not simply by a pious turn of speech that
Mary is called Queen of Apostles and Confessors; it is what
she truly is. Her life is the archetypal apostolic event (in so
far as there is an apostolate which is distinct from the mission
of Christ himself), of which all earlier apostolate is a shadow
and a forerunning (in the literal sense of the word), and from
which all later apostolate proceeds as a participation. So what
the apostolate is can be read from her and what she did; she
is a productive pattern for the apostolate, not a mere ideal
instance of its abstract essence.

Of course her life of apostolic mission and transmission of
salvation is historical, like everything else historical in God's
carrying-out of salvation; that is, being unique, concrete, historical, contingent it cannot be repeated and reproduced as it
was in its own unique time and place, in its own unique function in the totality of saving history. But on the other hand
we cannot separate the unique-historical element and the pro-
ductive-pattern element in this apostolate from each other,
like some substance and the accidents external to it; it is precisely in its historical uniqueness that the apostolate of the
Virgin Mother of the Divine Word is a living pattern for us.
Hence we do not need to be anxiously worried lest we "apply"
too much of what belongs to her apostolate to ourselves, and
thus exaggerate. If we look towards the apostolic life of the
Blessed Virgin, not only discussing it theoretically and analyzing it conceptually but approaching it in the direct contemplation and communication of faith, by which a Christian is

united with saving history in a grace-given anamnesis, then her apostolate will of itself take shape within us and our mission, as itself and yet in that fashion which will belong precisely to us and to our own time.

As in the life of Jesus, so in that of Mary, we have no right to ask why it should be just "like that"; no right to submit it to the forum of abstract conceptual morality, as though we were concerned only with those elements in it which can be established by us as individual applications of a general moral system discernible to us. The true apostolate is not the acceptance of some law discernible to us, *a priori,* about what the apostolate has to be like; it is the acceptance of that law of its being which we clearly perceive, in the first instance, in Mary. It is in this sense that all that is now going to be said must be understood, concerning the basic structure of all apostolate and all work for souls and their salvation, as we see it in the pattern of what that service was in Mary.

IV. The Basic Structures of the Apostolate and of Pastoral Work

1. Unity of the Apostolate of Clergy and Laity

In the first place, Mary's apostolate shows us the *unity of the apostolate of clergy and laity.* You cannot count Mary among the clergy, for though she is Queen of Apostles she is not in the liturgical and official sense a priest; but neither can you simply count her among "the laity," for, as we have already said, the position which she has among the redeemed is one of pre-eminence in the visible Church as such. Her task is an office, understanding by this a function within the public action of saving history; an office which claims the person for itself, whole and entire. Hence we may truly say that Mary is the living unity of the apostolate of clergy and laity; she is in a sense a living protest against all one-sided clericalism and one-sided laicism. To us clergy, she is saying: The Church's highest office—the most tangible function, most deeply entering into the flesh, that there is in the visible Church and in saving history at its most tangible—is an office proceeding from the Spirit; an office which can operate only by a living assent, integrating all that is personal into itself, made by the innermost center of the person.

She says to us clergy that office in the Church of the living Spirit is only truly and genuinely that which it needs and wills to be when it is also something personal, something undergone in grace and in love, something charismatic: when it does *not* fall comfortably back on the institutional element as though our official, authoritative commission, transcending all that is subjective, which exists and always will exist, were intended to excuse us from interior participation, from the profound imparting of our whole selves as subjective persons. The Church has always resisted all forms of false spiritualism— Donatism, Anabaptists ancient and modern, anti-clerical laicism in general—and defended the unqualified rights of the institutional element, objective sacraments, office, the clergy. But she has never done this in order to require less from us at the personal and charismatic level. She has done it while simultaneously venerating her who first conceived her Son (as the Fathers are always saying) in the spirit, in faith—in the subjective order, we might say—before she received him into her womb and bore him as, in his own person, the very objectivity of God's grace in this tangible world of space and time.

The Church has defended institution while at the same time acknowledging, in Mary, that the very highest official role that ever was or is in the Church is inseparably bound up with the holiness of the holy Virgin, with her personal, total belonging to God through her abiding sinlessness and perpetual virginity. The true defender of the rights of office is he who makes all such defense merely superfluous by the holiness with which he selflessly serves men through his office; who sees his office simply as a demand made by God upon himself as a person. He remains perfectly aware that the objective worth and validity of his preaching of the word, his administration of the sacraments, his pastoral authority is given to him so that he shall not despair at his own inadequacy, oppressed by the greatness of his mission; but he will never, like a pasha or a medicine-man, make his objective office and its powers into a weapon in the service of his own personal arrogance. For this objective office is rightly exercised and will fail to involve its holder in a heavier judgment only if, like the fire of sacrifice, it consumes him utterly in the service of his task towards men.

But Mary is equally a living pattern of contradiction towards any kind of laicism. For she became salvation to us only by the descent of the grace in her spirit bodily into her most blessed womb, by the objectivizing of that grace in the flesh of the Lord. It is the Spirit of God conceived from above and made truly concrete in this world of space and time which is the true Spirit: this is what is said to us by that reality which is the holy Virgin. Whereas all laicism is, at bottom, born of the notion that the Spirit does not need to be conceived, does not need to be made flesh, that his coming need not be in the humiliation of orders imposed from above and the conditioning of space and time; that his breath is anarchy. Let us simply point to the later life of the blessed Virgin as the model for the apostolate of the laity: her silence, her subordination to the legally prescribed religious life of her people, her self-effacement in the public life of her son, her standing beneath the cross (and not giving utterance to that lay resentment which says: Oh, so *now* I'm suddenly good enough to be on hand and stick my neck out); her unpretentious membership of the community at Pentecost, when she is, in herself, the central point, yet in no way detracts from the official rights of Peter and the Twelve. In short, her apostolate demonstrates the unity and reciprocal relationship between the official apostolate of hierarchical mission and the apostolate of personal service. Her apostolate tells us, the clergy, that even in the exercise of office the determining factor is holiness of service; it tells the layman that even the decisive role in redemption does not, *eo ipso,* include any title to or investment with the powers of office, that on the contrary it demonstrates its validity by leaving to office all its rights.

2. Unity in the Apostolate between Interior Spirit and Exterior Goal

We all suffer from the burdensome task of bringing personal interior holiness and external activity, *contemplatio* and *actio,* into a unity in the priestly life. We know that if we are not within ourselves men united to God, contemplatives, our apostolate will become sounding brass and tinkling cymbal; the work of a paid propagandist, who is really, at bottom, acting to protect himself and his source of income rather than to serve souls, and who hence does not, in the long run, deserve to be believed. But we also know the danger of trying to escape from the difficulties of the apostolate by quietly fleeing into peaceable, contemplative tranquillity: this may have been all right in the past, but today, when we are in the times of ultimate decision, it would be a sin against our mission. We know that words without heart become dead and empty; we know too that only too often when our own heart says what it needs must say it becomes empty.

Without the interior spirit our work is something dead; but how often the burden of the work weighs heavy on the spirit which yet, without the work, would be perverted into mere selfish feeling. The relationship between a holy interiority and external apostolic acts is like the relationship between body and soul: the soul would not be soul if it did not express itself as form in the bodiliness of its own exteriority, and at the same time this very body, which is the soul's creation, is also its burden and its peril.

This relationship between holy interiority and external hard work, between spirit and law, will always be a distressing problem for the apostle. Over and over again we shall realize that we have failed to do full justice to one or other of them, and so ultimately to both. It is possible to say very beautiful, profound and accurate things about this problem in theory, consoling and liberating things. But in practice we shall have to keep on putting up with the imperfection, inadequacy and sinfulness of our nature, here as elsewhere. Nothing short of our eventual consummation can be a complete remedy for this. But it is nevertheless important, stimulating and consoling for us to see, and to keep reminding ourselves, that the true relationship between these two things is not, fundamentally, a mutual antagonism; that they do not increase in inverse but in direct ratio; that they can reciprocally condition and benefit one another, at least in anyone who is called by God to the apostolate of external work, and hence whose vocation sends him forth into the exteriority of work without thereby taking from him the duty of interior holiness, which is only increased and made yet more binding by such a mission.

We see this reciprocally conditioning and beneficial relationship in the apostolate of the holy Virgin. The greatest act, the most real work of the whole of saving history, takes place within the silent chamber of a self-denying virgin at prayer; but all the holiness interior to this woman would have availed us nothing if the Spirit who overshadowed her had not become fruitful in her body. In her, act and spirituality are one. In her, interiority has no need to fear that it will be profaned and die when it issues forth in the external work of conceiving a child, serving him as a mother, submitting to a life of drudgery, enduring an oppressive political situation, walking the

way of the cross to its end. The spirit that was imparted to her
penetrates into this work; she obtains it by losing herself in
sheer, self-giving service of this work. Mary is so given over
to God that she can find him in everything: experience, prayer,
action, suffering. She is active in contemplation and contemplative in action. She can be both in one because of her will-
ingness to be always entirely at her master's service, because
she never seeks herself; because the very dualism of her life of
interiority and action issues from the One who totally disposes
of her; because that One wills and gives both, and hence the
dualism is not antagonism, not a "problem," but the many-
sidedness of one continuous doing of the will of the One whose
humble handmaid she is, always taking that which is here
and now being imparted to her.

When we look at Mary, we need have no fear that we shall
lose our souls if we allow ourselves to be consumed by our
work. Of course we shall defer to Christian prudence and
apportion our energies rationally. Of course we must not let
ourselves be perverted from missionaries and pastors into
modern managers and propagandists for an enterprise which
simply happens to be called the Church. Of course only that
which has been undergone by us, won in prayer and personally
believed, can ever really be preached. But if a man is unselfish
in service, humble in perseverance, compassionate, never disillusioned by all the disillusionments of his pastoral work, never
bitter and sceptical, always ready to be used to the utmost, silently and continuously consuming himself in the work of his
office, not seeking his own, but truly seeking others for their
own sake, then he need not fear that he is interiorly inadequate;
the action of his apostolate creates an infinite space within
him, a heart in which God establishes himself.

Such a man will indeed have to keep rekindling in himself,
by prayer and silence, that inner fire which alone can give
rise to such work. But he will also find that in a heart grown

empty in the selfless service of men interiority comes, as it were, of itself. He will find, with Mary, that the Child is nearest when he is no longer carried under one's heart but has been born into the world and has seemingly gone far off into the darkness of the Cross, leaving one with nothing but emptiness, night and a sense of failure. A man who has been called by the will of God and his Church to the pastorate, to word and work and life in the world, to bearing the weight of what seems like a godless state of affairs, to living in the diaspora, to a share in the bearing of the cross of failure, can confidently trust that in this work and this cross he will find God. The man who gives his life's blood in pastoral work will (to vary an old monastic saying) receive the Spirit of grace and strength and holiness as surely as if he had lived a contemplative life.

3. Unity in the Apostolate of Spirit and Norm, of Spirituality and Law

We of today, priests and people, have grown mistrustful of all the multitude of regulations and prescriptions in pastoral and apostolic work. We tend to get the impression that spirit, vitality, impetus and enthusiasm on the one hand, and a mass of official papers, canons, subsections and well-meant exhortations from above on the other do not necessarily increase in direct proportion. But when we look at Mary we find that we have to take fresh stock of our irritable scepticism about what is official, legal, apparently merely bureaucratic, a set of boardroom directives: and it stands revealed, in certain circumstances, as anything but spiritual, rather in fact sinful.

What was it that the Virgin did, what did she give us and communicate to us? The Spirit of God, who justifies us. Certainly. But by giving us the flesh of the Word, by giving to the infinite heavenly Word the very limited flesh of this earth.

Not by removing us from this world where everything is finite
and fixed and constricted, and this is not that, and there have
to be definitive norms; but by giving entrance to the spiritual
freedom of God precisely in this situation of flesh and law
and things laid down for us which we think we find unendur-
able. The true spirit of a true Christian apostolate is not a
spirit of anarchy, not the spirit of the "enthusiasts," but a
spirit which has the courage to submit to flesh, to concrete
precisions. And if in submitting it succumbs, i.e. dies, then
it simply proves that it is not the spirit of God. The courage
to be concrete, and hence to be precise, to be according to
norms, is an essential characteristic of the true spirit of the
apostolate. Worship of the letter may extinguish the spirit.
But what has at least as often been the death of the spirit is a
comfortably arbitrary devotion to merely general principles.

If the spirit is present only in the flesh of Christ and no
other way, then it is for us to have the courage (since we have
the duty) to ask ourselves at this conference what it means to
be apostolically and pastorally available to souls in really
solid and concrete terms, in a thoroughly fleshly way (we
might put it), in a thoroughly canonistic and legalistic way; to
ask ourselves what it means in the concrete when we say that
we, clergy and laity, must work together in our families and
places of work, in our parishes and in all cultural fields so
that the Word may enter into them and bear fruit. We must
grasp that *law is the body and flesh of the spirit;* we must be
able to recognize that distrust of norms laid down from above,
of things binding equally on everyone, of plans made in
common, is not simply a justified breadth of spirit but may be
Docetism in the pastoral field, a denial that the Word of God
has truly entered into our flesh; that it may be sinful pride
and disguised laziness. Wherever there is manifested among
the laity, today, a real apostolic energy and spirit of initiative,
there is an eagerness, what strikes us sometimes as an almost

fanatical eagerness, for carrying out concrete plans and clearly-defined tasks, for keeping account of what has been done, for concerted action and co-operation.

4. Further Basic Structures in the Marian Apostolate

(a) This apostolate is a mission from above. It is not something arrogated to oneself on one's own initiative; it is an undertaking, a service, a being claimed by a task which one has not given oneself, which in itself goes beyond one's own capabilities, in face of which one cannot but ask, "How shall this be done?"

(b) It is an apostolate with the capacity to wait for the right moment. It comes about when the time is fulfilled, when God appoints the hour for it. There are many things that ought to be; there is much which is in itself necessary, but it is not always, according to God's will, the right time for everything. The fact that a thing is good and holy in itself does not suffice to prove that it has a pressing claim on the limited energies now available. An all-embracing apostolate must be an apostolate which concentrates its energies on a few things, the things which are now urgent: upon the right *kairos*.

(c) Mary's apostolate is one of self-withdrawal behind the thing which she serves. She, among all human beings, performed the most decisive act in the whole of saving history. How little is said about it, even in the New Testament! How long a period was needed in Christendom before the all-surpassing scope and depth of Mary's assent came to be in some measure appreciated! The unnoticeable thing may be the most important; the snowball may become an avalanche; the Archimedean point of leverage is not always located at the spot where the loudest talk is going on. Courage to make an unimpressive start, the humility of small beginnings, is the charism of a truly great apostolate.

(d) Mary's apostolate is one of loyal perseverance in one and the same thing through all contingencies and situations. Mary really did only one thing: she conceived her son. Everything else was simply the unfolding of this single theme of her life. She did not merely say "Yes" once, in one great moment; she sustained that Yes, patiently, silently, constantly, in the serene assurance of the true believer, in the mature simplicity of real greatness, without repentance, like divine grace itself: sustained it throughout a whole lifetime. In the apostolate there have to be, at the right moment, ideas, plans, choices and decisions. But there does not have to be something new every year. What has been planted must be allowed to grow, what has been planned must be allowed to mature. Incessant experimentation would merely be a sign of weakness of faith and a dodging of hard work; a sign of that interior discontinuity which is a curse of our times. True, even in pastoral work we must always be converting ourselves to what is new, even here we must constantly be changing, because life means change and to be complete means to have changed often. But this change and this constant conversion must happen as an ever-renewed turning back to our one task, a perpetual reaffirmation of loyalty to a decision rightly made, a defeat of that emptiness and disgust which is forever laying hold on us sinful men even when we are engaged in the right task. May grace to overcome this temptation be obtained for us by the intercession of the mother of our Lord.

(e) The apostolate of the most blessed Virgin is an apostolate of the cross, of a heart stabbed through with the sword of suffering; an apostolate of failure, of bearing, with him, the destiny of her son; of noncomprehension of the decrees of God and of the actions of the Lord himself, whom she served. It is an apostolate of hope against hope, of faith before the victory is won, of a venture whose reward is not paid in advance, of a loyalty which gives all. Blessed art thou who hast believed, it was said to her. It could not have come more easily to her to believe in the salvation which was to come, as redemption, through her son than it does to us, at this moment of history, to believe that the truth remains: Christ yesterday, today, and the same forever. Christianity, if rightly grasped, must always seem improbable to the Christian. It is always the news which is to Jews a scandal and to Gentiles foolishness; it is always the power of God in the weakness of men, always a Church which seems to stand on the brink of collapse, and which seems, moreover, to be honestly doing her bit to make it so. There will always (as there were in the life of the holy Virgin) be a murderous Herod, godless priests, a cowardly Pilate, an apostatizing Peter, a people that longs for bread and not for grace, a conspiracy of silence and indifference, a rather primitive, inadequate sort of apostle, a rather old-fashioned, reactionary set of supporters (mostly pious women and other types not to be taken seriously); this will always be the situation, as it was with her, in which the apostolic act of faith has to maintain itself. And it is precisely in that moment when everything seems to be over and all seems lost that victory is won in defeat and life in death; the moment in which one stands up to receive the sword of deathly pain through one's heart, while the Son is praying his death-prayer of being forsaken by God.

5. Mary, the Guiding Pattern of Pastoral Work

I know that it may be said of all that I have been saying here that these are commonplaces and platitudes, not new and not helpful; that I have only repeated what everyone knows already and no one would seriously dispute. If this accusation refers to these things as *said,* then I accept it. But if it is supposed to apply to them as *heard,* then I reject it. I mean:

suppose that what has here been said remains really present to minds and hearts during our coming deliberations; that each of us applies these maxims not to his neighbor, so as to contradict him, but to himself, so as to sound the alarm in himself and to criticize himself, to lay his mind and his heart open to the ideas and proposals of his brothers in the priesthood; suppose that our discussions and our work proceed from this spirit as something really lived and not as something merely given an official approval: then might not all this, as something heard and really accepted, make an essential contribution to the success of our deliberations, well-known and undisputed though it may be?

If each one of us uses these long-recognized maxims as a weapon against his own mental laziness and the tepidity of his own heart; if A says to himself that the spirit without the concrete bodiliness of explicit rules is cheap anarchism (even though he hates all such prescriptions and is apt to put them aside as so much clutter of waste paper), while B tells himself that all rules without the spirit are dead and stay dead (even though he is really very much inclined to force his neighbors to follow in his own accustomed footsteps), then will not our deliberations be more fruitful than if each comes with the preconceived conviction that he has long possessed the pearl of wisdom in pastoral matters and has basically nothing more to learn? What so often makes conferences on pastoral theology so depressing and fruitless is that everyone gives an account of his own maxims and virtues and recommends them as the best possible recipe to everybody else. So if we submit ourselves to that guiding pattern of pastoral work which we can discern in the image of the Queen of Apostles and Cause of our Joy as redeemed Christians, if each one of us does this, thinking not of someone else but of himself, then a Morning Star, the Morning Star of grace, will shine upon our counsels.

V. Bold Adaptation to Our New Situation

Finally, there is something else that we should not forget. It is true that every age has thought that it was a new age such as had never been before. But it is nevertheless true that we are, historically, in the midst of a *breaking up of things* which does, in many important respects, involve lumping together all past periods as one by contrast with that which is approaching. I do not hesitate to say that we do not over- but underrate the profundity and extent of this break-up. We may try to characterize the coming age in different ways in our philosophy or theology of history. We may hail it as the dawn of the true age of man or fear it (or long for it) as the beginning of the end. But this we can say at any rate: An epoch is beginning in which man is emancipating himself to a degree inconceivable hitherto from the restrictions and the protecting guardianship of nature, from circumstances which have simply grown and not been made. Nature, meaning the salutary compulsions of what cannot be avoided—one's native environment, the laws of the body, the characteristics of materials as nature produces them, etc.—protects man against himself and his *hubris*. Today man has successfully set about a far-reaching conquest of nature, and in the same instant he has fallen a prey to himself and to the demons within his own breast. He has to learn to protect himself. He has first to grasp that anything he *can* do is not necessarily something that ought to be done; that what is possible is not necessarily what is prescribed and wholesome.

As for how an experiment such as man is now making with himself will turn out, we do not know. But as for the fact that in such a situation he has got himself into a crisis over faith, society, morals and every other dimension of his being, that is not really particularly astonishing. So if, in such an age, our pastoral work seems outwardly to have a very defensive character, if we are only with difficulty keeping unchristian forces

at bay, if we are only with difficulty feeling our way forward
in pastoral questions, if we are in a period of endurance rather
than of perceptible victory, of defense rather than of established possession, all this is not really very astonishing. It does
not in the least mean that we haven't a chance, that we are
inevitably bound to go down and down. Every courageous
adaptation to the new situation, small though it may be, every
position held, every new Christian won in the teeth of all the
difficulties, every pastoral insight, however small, may well be
a great victory, seen from a higher level and judged as a part
of long-term development; for this may all be a preparation
for the time when, once humanity has acclimated itself to the
new age, once it has to some degree settled down in it, Christianity will once again appear, even in unintelligent eyes, as
what it is: the religion which unites us to God the true and the
living, and which possesses the promise of eternity.

Hence, again, we should not think too slightingly of our
momentary undertakings. Anything we do is of course only
one small factor in a world-wide spiritual event which goes
beyond our sight: the battle between the empire of sin and the
grace of God. But in such a battle, whose decision is for
eternity, how can anything be really small and unimportant if
it is done because God wills it and because we must do what
little we can? Is it of no account, if we simply come to realize
a little about the specific character of the Catholic apostolate
and direct our actions accordingly? Is it unimportant if we
become more conscious, these days, that pastoral theology and
the practical care of souls are a participation in the unutterable mystery of the love and power of God in history; that we
are not a sort of propaganda agents for some kind of spiritual
business-concern but ambassadors of God, commissioned by
him once for all? If we reach a better understanding of what
the words "pastoral" and "apostolate," both of priests and
laity, involve on all levels of human existence, and translate
it sensibly and accurately into concrete decisions and terms

of reference; if we do this with clarity, submissiveness, mutual understanding and the confidence of faith; if in all this there shines upon us the Morning Star of redemption, the image of the Queen of Apostles, so that we are conscious that we are continuing what she began, and hence that the law of her actions and her sufferings is also the law of our apostolate, then this conference will have been a blessing indeed.

5

THE SACRIFICE OF THE MASS
AND AN ASCESIS FOR YOUTH

Two Preliminary Points

1. This is a difficult theme, because the sacrifice of the Mass is an entity with very many dimensions. Moreover it is a mystery, the *mysterium fidei,* as all-embracing and immeasurable as the whole reality and truth of salvation itself. This alone is enough to make it plain that one can always affirm and bring to the fore new aspects of the Church's sacrifice. And on the other hand, man too is an endlessly many-levelled and many-dimensional creature, not only when considered statistically but also in terms of his individual and supra-individual history. It follows from this simple fact that it is always possible to bring fresh aspects of man into contact with fresh and different aspects of the Mass. There is no end to the combinations that arise between particular human needs, tasks, attitudes and endeavors at all the various stages of life on the one hand, and aspects of this central, all-embracing mystery of Christianity on the other. Hence it must be expected, *a priori,* that the problem posed here admits of an endless series of fresh answers.

It is clear from the start that none of them can claim to be the one right answer. Indeed, the history of eucharistic devotion and of the part played in the Church by the sacrifice and sacrament of the altar show what great changes have affected man's relationship to the Mass. This is not only a fact but a legitimate fact. For one must beware of condemning all these various and genuinely Christian ways of treating the Eucharist. One must not take one's own form of practice, which may be very good and may indeed accord very closely with the Holy Spirit at this particular time of the Church's life, and try to prove, on dogmatic grounds, that it is the one and only right and salutary one. Dogmatic discussion is always useful and necessary for the criticism and justification of religious practice. But one must beware of thinking that if only one has a deep and fundamental grasp of dogma one can deduce from it the absolutely right way of conducting one's religious practice, now and forever. No such thing. In all these questions all we can do is think about dogma (which also has a history, to the progress of which all such discussions make their own contribution) and about our own pastoral experience and our own intimate knowledge of ourselves and our times in concrete historical terms (for in these factors too the guidance of the Church's Spirit makes itself felt), and consider what is best to be done: how we, from our side, can approach more closely to the one mystery, forever new, of the only living God in Jesus Christ; how we can most quickly become devout. We cannot and need not do more. Whenever dogma seeks to lay down the one and only salutary course for devotion and for pastoral practice, it has thereby failed to grasp the nature of its own tasks and potentialities and those of its time. It is then presuming itself fit to make an exhaustively adequate analysis of real religious life, in the concrete (both in the individual's own life and in his pastoral work); the theologians are oppressing the prophets and men of the spirit. But this does not work, and brings nothing but disaster. This is not to deny that dogma does have a normative role in pastoral work and Christian pedagogy; but it is a limited role.

This, then, is something that we do not want, from the outset, to forget. We must not think that there is any single solu-

tion attainable, *a priori*, to such questions. At any particular
period, any particular time of life and in any particular environment, there may well be one particular form of, for
example, eucharistic life which is really the right one, able to
be an historical force, really productive of religious life, du-
rably strong and in a certain sense, for that particular time,
typical. But in the last analysis the individual has to find this
for himself. Life is something that the Church in her concrete
devotion *discovers;* what the theologian does is rather to
reflect upon it when it is already there. This is something that
follows from the nature of things, from the relationship between the Church, her life, and the reflections of theology. So
you must not be surprised if you do not now find yourselves
listening to prescriptions for patent remedies.

2. The second point is this: the Mass is not Christianity.
In all ages, and today especially, there are people whose one
desire is for a single, unique formula. They want the one idea,
the one solution, the one all-embracing recipe in religious
matters. Simplification and reduction to a few fundamental
ideas and positions are good things. Along with the periods
of expansion and Baroque lavishness there are always times
in the history of thought which are periods of intellectual concentration and reduction, of simplicity, classicism and the
uncluttered line. But one must not exaggerate; especially not
in matters of religion and Christianity. Neither devotion to the
Sacred Heart nor devotion to Mary nor devotion to the Holy
Ghost nor yet the Mass can simply be the basic formula or
the single organizing principle for the whole of religious life.
Not even the Mass. True, it is a most central mystery of
Christian existence. Why this is so does not need to be explicitly stated here. But we only need to consider one point in
the first instance: Cult-sacrifice and sacrament exist primarily
(*in recto*) in the dimension of *sign,* of expression, of tangibility in the historic and social order. They are primarily the
sign of the thing, not the thing itself; the sign of what is cen-

tral, not that central thing itself. They do indeed contain what they signify: Christ, his grace, the covenant, the atonement, eternal life, the fullness of glory. But what they signify is given, precisely, only under this one sign.

According to the Council of Trent the Eucharist is the incomparable sacrament. But there are other sacraments too, and they also contain what they signify, which is this selfsame grace. And that which is made present in all the sacraments in an effective sign is not thus made present because it would not otherwise be present in the world at all. That which is signified in this and in all the sacraments and made present by the effective, "exhibitive" word of the sacraments is also present and effective elsewhere in Christian living: in the act of a believing heart, in conversion, in fidelity, in patience in suffering, in hoping against hope, in what we call sanctifying grace and supernaturally elevated acts of grace. The threefold God dwells in men's hearts; he has bound us to the sacraments, but he has not bound himself and his grace to the sacraments. His Spirit breathes where he will, and we know, as Christians, that he wills to breathe through all the by-ways of our being, that his kingdom wills to come everywhere, that everything is meant to become a realization of his atonement and his holy coming.

Christianity is not only in the Church, not only in the sacraments, not only in the cult. It is always and everywhere. And not only in the sense that it is meant to work outwards into everything; not only in the sense that we are meant to go out from the altar into every dimension of our being and every aspect of our lives so as to work out in a Christian life the grace received at the altar. That is so too, but that is not all. The reception and increase of this same grace can happen and is meant to happen in Christian *life* itself. We are meant to come back from our lives to the altar full of the grace given to us through those lives, because it is only thus, coming from life to the altar, that we are able and worthy to do what must be done there. Christian life pours itself into the altar, just as it proceeds from it.

Hence it is wrong to proclaim the Eucharist as the one and only source of Christian life and grace. We cannot even say, *a priori*, that it is certain that God must, in each and every case, bestow the decisive high points of our life upon us in this sacramental event. The most deep and intimate communion with God in Christ is not always bound to be sacramental communion. For the Council of Trent says that it is also possible to receive the grace of the Eucharist (the thing itself) in spiritual communion. If, then, spiritual communion is more than a merely subjective desire for something which is not in fact given at all (Denzinger 881), this means recognizing the non-sacramental life of grace with a definiteness and clarity which calls for more attention from theologians and pastors. Because God is all in all; because he wills to integrate everything into his kingdom and his grace; because there is no principle binding upon him to say how he must, in practice, effect the decisive acts of his mercy and sanctification in men by his grace: we must not set about acting as though the Mass were the absolute, univocal central point of religious life, from which everything has to proceed and to which everything must be reduced. God is the only central point. And that center is everywhere. True, this is not to deny that God himself has made certain focal points and centers of gravity for us finite creatures, and that we must abide by them. Hence it does not imply any absolute structureless chaos in our Christian existence. But it is a consideration which warns us against falling into religious monomania.

If we look at the history of the Church and of the saints (i.e., of the authentic representatives of Christianity), and especially at the history of the first Christian centuries, we shall have to say that what has just been dogmatically stated here is also affirmed by history. Despite a romantic exuberance manifested here and there in the liturgical movement, by which the sacrifice of the Mass is exalted and allotted a central position in history, the Mass never has been so absolutely the center of all Christian existence that everything had to proceed from it and be referred back to it. The Christian, because he accepts God as always One who is greater than all else, has never been a person for having just one idea, one method, one absolute way. The saints were strikingly unsystematic people in their lives: people enthralled by God the Absolute and yet with a love for St. Joseph; already living a mysticism beyond images, and yet at the same time staunch churchmen; building their lives upon Jesus Christ and yet having a devotion to the angels, etc.

This is what justifies something that sometimes strikes us as irritating and rhetorical in dogmatic and ascetical literature: the habit of speaking in such vast and splendid terms about some one thing, as though it were the one and only thing that mattered, and then on some other occasion lauding some other thing again, as though the whole of salvation depended upon that. Take Pope Pius XII: he praises Mary as though today everything depended upon her; he writes an encyclical about the Sacred Heart as though it were the most important thing of all; no doubt he praised both religious congregations and third orders as though there were nothing in the world dearer to his heart than each of them in turn. We do not have to have any special liking for these alternations, as far as we ourselves are concerned. But they do embody the impartiality of a Christian man, who can lovingly enfold many things in his embrace without seriously thinking that any one of them is, in all literalness, the one and only absolute of religious life. And this is something of which we have to think when we talk about the Mass. If we do not do this in practice; if, with well-meaning zeal, we make the Mass into an absolute in our religious life, as though there were no such things as prayer and action and private interior life and subjective penance and a world and its work and one's occupations and one's joys as well, or as though each and every thing had to be explicitly related to the Mass—then we might indeed for a while improve our success in religious pedagogy, because of the limpid clarity and taut, linear logicality in our system for living. But the whole thing would be fundamentally false, and falsity does not survive in the long run. We should be cutting off the people we instruct from possibilities in their religious life to which they have a right; we should be doing them damage in the long run, because we should be blocking possibilities which might be the only ones by which they could come to a healthy realization of their own Christianity.

This is, of course, not to say in the very least that the Mass is a mere item in Christianity, merely something among all its countless possibilities, events and actions, such as devotion to the angels, indulgences, St. Aloysius' Sundays, etc. Quite obviously we can and must work at our religious education so as to bring Christian youth to realize the Mass for what it is: the *mysterium fidei,* the climax of the cult that honors God in the holy community of those who are chosen by the calling of Christ, the celebration of the redemption, the anamnesis of that death which gave us life, the uniting of us with the Body of the Lord as the pledge of our liberation from guilt, of our strength for daily living, of the unity of the Church, the resurrection of the body, the glorification and eternal acceptance of the world, the presence of God never again to be taken from us. The Mass can and must be very central indeed. We can most certainly work in this direction. Indeed (and much more today than in earlier times) the standardized type of Christian (which is something necessary and unavoidable within mass education) actually should put the Mass in the center and make it, quite seriously, the essential point of his religious life. This is necessary because today, in these times when men are so stretched and tormented and overdriven, we cannot afford to go out to the periphery of humanity to seek that divine wholeness which, in itself, may be found anywhere, even though it may quite well be there (and could be found there more easily in earlier times than is possible today). But while this is true, and this truth is our underlying assumption in all that we are trying to do here, yet we must not be one-sided, we must not do our teaching as though a young Christian living his life had nothing but the possibility of drawing on the Mass or else getting nothing at all; we must not try officiously to deduce everything from the Mass and reduce everything to it. Objectively, such things are always logically possible; so are the efforts of those mentally ingenious and personally limited people who construct systems of religious life in which it is demonstrated that so long as one honors the Mother of God everything else automatically falls into place. But subjectively and existentially, monomanias of this sort are false and dangerous. Even when they pick on the Mass as their object.

The Mass in the Totality of Christian Life

After making these two preliminary points, let us approach the theme itself.

First of all there is something to say which can be reckoned as basically part of our theme, or might equally be included in the prologomena. Our theme being the Mass and an ascesis for youth, it goes without saying that we have to be fairly clear about the relationship between sacrament, *opus operatum*, the objective cult-action of the community on the one hand, and subjective devotion and personal choice on the other. It is a truth of faith, not a piece of modern subjectivism, that the *opus operatum*, the sacrament, the cult-action has its meaning, value, significance and effectiveness only in so far as it is integrated in the person's own indispensable, irreplaceable subjectivity, at least when the person, not being an infant, is capable of such acts. One can receive grace through a sacrament only if and in proportion as one disposes oneself, by grace, to receive that grace (Denzinger 798, 819, 850, 898, 914). Sacraments are not there to act as substitutes for what needs to be subjectively performed by a person: for his faith, his conversion, his internal consent to God and his grace, his acceptance of existence in its subjection to death, his hope in life in the midst of death; neither to substitute for them nor to make them less exacting. That is not the nature of the sacraments. By and large, moreover, this is clear enough and taken for granted even in standard textbook theology.

But there are recurrent points where this clarity is obscured. Here and there (consider some of the conclusions drawn from the adequacy of imperfect contrition in the sacrament of penance) there is a recurrent temptation, sometimes even in practice, to let it be tacitly implied that the sacraments were instituted to lighten for us and relieve us at least in part of the duty of total personal decision. It is said, e.g., that apart from confession you have to have perfect contrition, while with confession imperfect contrition is enough. This is to forget that imperfect contrition is actually the difficult element in perfect contrition, and that even a man who has been absolved cannot ultimately be saved unless he really loves God in the way required for perfect contrition. It is said, e.g., that less aversion for sin is required in order to have punishment remitted by an indulgence than by the sacrament of penance. All such subcutaneous tendencies in theology should be radically resisted. Ultimately, God wills and endorses the sacraments and everything else objective in the cult and in the Church only in order that man shall give him his own subjectivity, his heart. He offers man his grace through the sacraments, he places it at his disposal; but his grace becomes man's salvation only if man accepts it, putting it subjectively into operation, and only in precisely that degree to which he does so.

If it becomes impossible to achieve a fair measure of subjective appropriation and subjective realization of the Mass and the sacraments (that is, to the increase of faith, hope and love), then these cult-events cease, to that same degree, to be meaningful and pleasing to God. The Mass still continues to be the objective making present of the sacrifice of Christ on the Cross, it is still the act of Christ the High Priest; but since cult-sacrifice, within the dimension of cult, has no significance as a formal honoring of God without an interior sacrificial intention, and since the act of Christ's interior intention as High Priest is not increased by multiplication of Masses but remains one and the same act of that intention which has become eternal, it follows that each new Mass is indeed, absolutely speaking, an honoring of God, but that it involves an *increase* in the formal honoring of him, i.e. in that honor which can only be paid by the subjective acts of spiritual persons, only if and in so far as the honoring of him is extended among men, the members of the Church, who can only honor him, really and ultimately, in so far as they bring their whole existence as believers to enter into and realize that which they perform in the cult. The sacraments of themselves make the offer of grace. But this grace has to be accepted. And acceptance, in an adult, does not mean the mere performance of the sacrament plus a purely passive nonresistance on the part of the person, but a believing, hoping and loving acceptance (with growth in all three) of the sacramental event. If there is no growth in this interior disposition (even though it be not the cause but the condition of sacramental grace), neither is there any growth in grace as really conveyed by the sacrament and the sacrifice. From this, only briefly indicated here, there follows as part of our actual theme:

The "Living of Life" and the "Church's Mass"

Education directed to the Mass and the altar must not be merely education in what belongs to cult and community. Liturgical education is part of Christian education and formation. But this in turn essentially involves education in personal prayer, self-denial, doing one's duty in life, offering silent sacrifice, accepting, as a lonely human being, one's own non-transferable responsibility: in short, an education for the totality of a Christian life and death. It is only where such education takes place that there is any real education in the Mass. For it is only to the extent that this happens and is achieved that we have a person who is capable of doing sacramentally that which is done under the sign of the cult only in order that it may be done better in life itself, and in order that what is done in life may be given, in the cult, an historical-sacramental tangibility and embodiment. In other words: unless the *res sacramenti* happens in a person's life, unless the whole fullness and breadth of a Christian education is directed towards this end, the *sacramentum* of the Mass will be in vain, and there will be no appropriation through the *sacramentum* of its *res*. Unless the Lord's coming, his ever-present parousia, his life and death, are being celebrated in a person's life, there is no meaning in their cult-celebration. Education for the altar, thus understood, is also education stemming from the altar, for what happens at the altar does indeed require that a person bring his life, formed in Christ, to the altar as a holy oblation, so that the offering of that life which, in Christ and with him, is made in life itself may also be given, in the cult, that clear statement, that sacramental immediacy, which heightens it and makes it visible.

But it would still be wrong to try to draw the whole of such an education in lines leading to and from the altar. It would result in merely artificial constructions; it would be a hindrance to a fundamental, interior understanding of these things in themselves. Prayer, meditation, self-discipline, love for the Crucified, fidelity to one's vocation, readiness to help others can all no doubt receive fruitful stimulus from the Mass. But it all has to be understood and practiced in itself in the first instance, grasped existentially according to its own necessity, if a young person is ever really to make it his own. It is only with this extra-liturgical education in Christian living that a person really becomes capable of celebrating the sacrifice of the Mass with interior, existential participation. And in so far as this formation in Christian living is to be conceived and carried out as an education enabling one personally to perform the act of the Mass, what is necessary is to discover and make use of those potentialities in human life which bear a special affinity to what happens in the Mass.

What is needed is an awakening, activating and deepening of understanding for the inconceivable majesty of that mystery which reigns over and in our lives and which we call God; we must find a maieutic method of instructing another person in what it really means to adore God, and in general to realize him; there must be an education towards a valid, spontaneous achievement of all that is meant by thanksgiving, acknowledgment of God, self-surrender, contrition. For all these things, we must search out the point of insertion in concrete life, the point at which something of this nature really and spontaneously arises in man. And it simply is not to be supposed that it is always possible for this point to be the Mass itself; the Mass may well be far too emphatically the great, solemn, liturgical, communal act for it to be possible really to grasp what is happening in it unless one has already come to understand all this through some other experience of a more simple, personal nature. The silly phrase that people use about worshipping better under the blue dome of heaven than at Mass has its kernel of genuine truth: you have to be devout before you can be devout at Mass.

This is not to be taken in an exclusive sense, but it is true. Instruction in personal prayer, the practice of meditation, of silence, and other things of the same sort are necessary or useful preparations for a more intensive participation in the Mass. But if our teaching fails to induce a growing personal participation, then people who do not have the sociological support and framework that we clergy have in this matter will soon cease to understand why they should be present at Mass at all. Just ask yourself honestly: Do you yourself have a need, a real, genuine need of the Mass, and does this need operate when you are seeking God really personally, or indeed when you are seeking him at all—do you too get the impression that on very many occasions and very many days you would do quite well without it? Having asked ourselves this, we may perhaps be in a position to gauge how much it really involves to have, interiorly, right of access to the frequent celebration of Mass. But we need to have such access, these days, or neither formal obedience to the Church nor the divine commandment itself will go on much longer having any effect on the laity.

Summing up: The "Mass of life" is a necessary condition for the "Mass of the Church." It is only by educating people for the one that we can educate them for the other. And without the Mass of life the Mass at the altar cannot be celebrated in such fashion that it is really what it ought to be, namely the sacramental embodiment of the Mass of life, which itself also grows by being incarnated in the cult.

Education for Interior Actualization

What we have to demand is *personal participation* in the Mass. Simply to join in performing the actions of the cult by a liturgical participation of words, singing, etc., is not enough to achieve that interior disposition which is the necessary condition if the *mysterium Christi* is to take place in the Mass not only as an objective event but in the hearts of men, which is what it exists for. The most perfectly celebrated Mass is that in which faith, hope, love, heart-felt gratitude, adoration of God from the innermost core of one's being and receptiveness to his pardoning grace are most fully realized. It follows from this that all our training in liturgy and everything that we arrange in this field must always be judged by the test of whether it really and honestly serves that interior actualization. If we organize something splendid in the way of liturgy because otherwise the young folk will get bored with Mass and won't know what to do with themselves, we are only dodging the difficulty and our real task: which is to introduce them so deeply into the mysteries which take place within man— prayer, awe in the presence of God—that they simply will not be bored at Mass, even if it be a silent Mass with "nothing happening."

Of course I am not saying anything against making efforts to keep the young people reasonably occupied and to make the service attractive and interesting for them (this both could and should be done even more than it is, and the liturgical movement, as a truly pastoral enterprise, has not yet achieved anything like what should be done in this respect). Nor am I saying anything against the idea, which is right, that liturgy properly performed (if and in so far as it is properly celebrated by people who have been educated in it) may be the best form for the best and easiest self-realization of the spirit of a true Christianity of the heart. We will readily admit that the fact that an inferior external performance of the liturgy, given that it is really entered into, can produce a greater interior religious effect is no argument against a better performance, a more large-scale, correct and polished celebration, which may often fail to be "devotional" (as is charged against it) for no other reason than that it has not been properly and patiently entered into. But it still remains true and crucial that if education in the Mass is not an education in interior participation in what happens at it, and if the external presentation of the ceremony (which is a part of that education) makes this harder rather than easier, then the education is wrong.

The more you value the Mass as a concentrated essence of the whole of Christianity, the more you must educate people for the Mass outside the Mass, by educating them for the whole of Christianity, which is something more than liturgy. And this cannot be done if you try to do it only in connection with the Mass. But when actual explicit education and formation in the celebration of Mass is being done, even this must not consist more or less exclusively of instruction in the liturgical action as such, the *sacramentum,* but must always aim at being an education and formation directed towards the *res sacramenti.*

Education in the Mass and an Ascesis for Youth

Perhaps everything said so far has been confined too much to the general and obvious. It may be so. I do not wish to dispute it, though I think that these obvious points are still being constantly forgotten in practice. However that may be, we come now to a further section of our theme, a question which will, I think, take us into the heart of it. I mean the quest for a Christianity and an ascesis specific to young people, and a correspondingly specific aspect of the celebration of the Mass. By young people I do not here mean children, but people who are on the one hand no longer children and on the other do not yet have the sense, with so-called adults, of the burden of life and the oppressiveness of death but are still growing up, people to whom this life is still all promise: young people between the ages of fifteen and twenty-five. To make really clear what is to be said, this needs to be somewhat expanded.

The Phases of Religious Life

It is obvious that human life goes through not only biological phases, stages of development, but spiritual ones as well, and that man's being a body-spirit means that the two of course go together. Each of these phases has its own special stamp, its own irreplaceable character, its own unique significance, its own particular weight, and no other phase can be a substitute for it. And all of them build up together, reaching out through their successors, towards the consummation, which lies beyond our empirical reach, of a complete and resurrected human being. If such phases exist at the spiritual-personal level, they necessarily do at that of religion. But if even at the religious level these phases have the characteristics which we have just indicated, there follows another obvious truth which is always being forgotten: certain religious manifestations have their right and proper place at one particular phase of life and not at another. Not everything in religion has its due time at every stage of life; not everything can be performed, genuinely and spontaneously, in every phase.

Of course it is not that certain religious phenomena are plainly and simply not *there* in a given religious phase, and simply do not need to be there. This is not what is meant. Not only do we have the phenomenon of those who are (in a good sense) precocious in religious development, and the phenomenon (belonging particularly and rightly to the spiritual sphere) that the tempo of maturation and fulfilment does not simply coincide with the tempo and rhythm of physical and biological time. There is also the fact that in the mind and heart of man everything is always present all at once, and hence can always be mediated to him and cultivated in him (and even, to a certain extent, must be). But it is not always present in the same mode, with the same explicitness, fullness and intensity, as regards actually putting it into operation. Everyone, for example, has some kind of experience of the vulnerability and frailty of existence, the sense of insecurity. But the acceptance and endurance of this element in human existence takes place differently at each stage of life, more or less piercingly, more or less explicitly, in varying manners, so that at the different stages of one person's life there arise, within what is always the same humanity, altogether incommensurable realizations of one's being.

Co-ordination of Phases with Religious Truths

Of course this has always been known in some sense, nor, in all probability, is it really denied in practice by any religious educator. But I will make the assertion that too little notice is taken of it in ecclesiastical practice in religious matters; the phenomenon is not seen clearly enough nor its importance discerned. Just consider, quite simply, the following: in the ecclesiastical regulation of the conduct of life according to the Code of Canon Law there are, it is true, a few requirements from which one is exempted before the age of seven, or of twenty-one, and after the age of fifty-nine. But by and large a person's age is of practically no account in the rules and prescriptions which shape Christian living. As far as the great mass of ecclesiastical directives goes, as soon as children cease to be children in the narrower sense they begin to be regarded simply as undifferentiated Christian people. And to my mind the fact that you here are pastorally charged with the care of growing youth above the age of childhood is the exception that proves the rule. If we look at religious history in general, we shall see that this levelling practice is not simply something to be taken for granted.

Why do we not have a monasticism specifically intended for that age when life is biologically behind us, and hence can, on that assumption, begin at last to be really lived spiritually? Does it really go without saying that at twenty-four a man becomes a presbyter, an "elder"? Why is there no longer an "order" of widows? Is it not conceivable that one may perhaps, without realizing it, in the case of a man in the plenitude of his powers, when his life is focused upon this world and its secular tasks, face him with religious demands which at that stage, a possibly legitimate period of religious latency, are excessive; and that one is thus (because he feels guilty about it) cutting him off even at a later time of life from what could then have been unfettered religious practice? Plenty more

such questions could be asked. They would all envisage widely
differing aspects of the problem of differentiated religious practice according to age, as it ought in theory to be.

This variation, necessary in itself and profoundly far-reaching, in how religion is put into practice according to a person's
spiritual age does not only affect certain practices and modes
of behavior. The phenomenon is also relevant to our relationship to religious truths. Of course what is true is true always
and for everybody. Obviously, since later on religious instruction and true initiation into the reality of Christianity will
not be possible to a sufficient degree, one will try somehow,
as best one can, to introduce the child and the adolescent
mentally to the whole of that reality. But this does not alter
the fact that it is not only a question of a childish, a youthful
and an adult notion of the whole of that doctrine, in each of
which, though in their own way, the individual items of the
faith are all grasped with an equal degree of explicitness and
existential intimacy. There is also a closer or more distant
existential relationship to the different truths at different ages,
a greater or lesser possibility of realizing them, stronger or
weaker receptive faculty. Responsiveness to particular truths
does not only vary with individuals, it also changes from one
age to another. This really is a platitude.

But as soon as we ask ourselves: Would I be able to say
exactly which of the truths appearing in our catechism are pre-
eminently appropriate, intimately congenial and assimilable at
each particular stage of growth?—then we are probably not
ready with an answer. But this shows that we have never really
and precisely thought out these obvious points. But they will
not become usable in our religious pedagogy until we have
thought them out precisely and investigated their consequences. We might ask, for instance: Is there a particular age
which is especially trinitarian? Is there a particular age which
perhaps recapitulates the collective phase of the Old Testament, so that (by analogy with biological theory) ontogenesis

recapitulates phylogenesis? Is there a specifically "ethical" age in human life? Is it possible that even in this life one's interior affinity with the sacramental system may slowly diminish, as a prelude to eternity, in which there will be no sacraments? Such questions and many others could be asked if we want to get a clearer and more precise idea of the separate ages of religion, not only in their manner of practice but also in their theoretical relationship to the individual truths and realities of faith.

Of course it would also have to be done with reference to particular forms of devotion. One may, for example, set a very high value on devotion to the Sacred Heart and regard it as one of the deepest, most intimate and most existential secrets of grace in the Christianity of our times. But one may nevertheless wonder whether one can or should introduce such things not only at all stages of religious development (which, while connected with age-levels, are not identical with them) but also at each and every age? It may be doubted whether a young person can get on with it at all. Not because he is more rational or more enlightened or more concerned with essentials than certain devout people, but because he cannot as yet grasp it. For he is simply not capable yet of seeing the ultimate mystery of the world, of the redemption and of his own being in terms of the foolish prodigality of love. It is not a valid objection to say that the Church recommends it (and many similar things) to all. For it would have to be proved, which could certainly not be done, that the recommendation was really intended indiscriminately. It would have to be proved that any general cult in the Church as a whole involves and requires an explicit, emphatic performance of it on the part of each individual, which equally could not be proved, because the contrary is true. Nor, finally, must one forget that it simply is not the case that everything sublime, only intelligible to the wise and mature, gets displayed in the market-place and at some period in the Church's history distorted into something mass-produced for each and every individual and age-group. This has applied even to voluntary self-flagellation.

Youth and Its Understanding of the Mass

What follows for our theme? That what has been said applies equally to the religious attitude of the young in relation to the Mass, and to the Mass in relation to the young. It follows, for instance, that we should be doing the wrong thing if we tried to introduce a young person to this mystery by the same door through which we ourselves enter into it. It would be wrong to try to develop a symmetrical dogmatic structure involving as many exalted points of view as possible and impose it on a young person as completely and comprehensively as we could. Of course we do have to try, at this age, to sow the seeds which will grow later on into a relationship to the Mass corresponding to a later age. But to implant potentialities which will for the time being remain very largely latent is a very different thing from bringing into action a Christian reality in as developed a form as possible, corresponding to a person's age at this moment. And it seems to me that we need to pay attention to this even when teaching about the Mass.

It is not possible (for evident reasons) to discern directly from the Mass itself which precise aspects of it are congenial to this age, so that they can be specially cultivated and, moreover, made into a special point of departure for the education and conduct of Christian life as a whole. For the Mass has aspects for every age-group and does not itself directly indicate which aspects apply to which particular age-group. The question of which image of the Mass is directly accessible to the young is one that must be answered by reference to the special character of youth. If this were done, if one could discover a theology of the Mass existentially accommodated to the special religious character of this age, then there would be a correspondence between what is done in the Mass and what is done in life. Then the Mass could be the sacramental embodiment of what really happens in these lives, and not merely of what appears, as equally binding on all, in the pages of the catechism. The inward and outward working of life into the Mass and Mass into life would then go better.

As, from these very abstract considerations, we thus develop a program of what needs to be done, we do not, Heaven forbid, mean to suggest that it has never been seen before or never been tackled and achieved. Pedagogical theory always limps along behind life. And there are always plenty of practical teachers, thank God, doing things even though they have never heard of them and have not yet explicitly reflected upon them. I am sure that this is the case to a large extent here. But if one does reflect upon the problem and grapple with it more clearly, this can be useful too. And here, then, we have a job for those who are actually pastors of youth, not for the dogmatic theologians. For it is they who can and must be in a better position to say what the young people whose souls are entrusted to them really are like.

The considerations presented here have no more to add than this: question your knowledge of these young people quite explicitly. From which direction does such a person need in fact to find his way to the Mass, and from which would he be bound to find it difficult and impossible? On which truths concerning this sacrifice am I going to touch to such an extent that I may hope that after a long wait, lying as though dead in the furrows of the soul, these seeds may at last in a quite different stage of life spring up and bear fruit? And of which truths can I speak here and now in such fashion that they will here and now be spirit and life? Considerations of this kind are not superfluous, if it makes any sense at all to reflect about religious pedagogy. So we will now say something about these questions, even though at this point the dogmatic theologian needs to give way to the superior competence of the educator and religious teacher.

The "Youthful" Christian

So the first thing is to say something about youth and its religious life in general, and then to see what consequences follow in relation to one's conception and performance of the Mass and how this can and ought to react upon one's life. And though we shall not be able to say anything new here about young people, nevertheless we cannot go on without saying anything on the subject, since this is the immediate basis for answering our actual question.

Youth is optimistic. A person at this age has his life before him. It has not yet disillusioned him, it is still on the upgrade. He is more aware of possibilities than of limitations. He has begun to take possession of himself; he is aware of himself as a person who is his own task and his own reward. Hence he is an *ethical person* in a special sense of the word. Ethical problems interest him because they are directly connected with what he is experiencing at precisely this time, namely the independent construction of his own life. Hence religious questions and undertakings will appeal to him under an ethical aspect. Further, a young person is oriented towards the world, especially in the case of a boy; he seeks to fulfil himself in some objective, measurable achievement such as can be pointed out to other people, not in an interior savoring of life. Hence, for instance, the special interest in sport at this age. A young person is, if one may put it this way, the champion in an optimistic *agon:* he sees life as a battle, but not so much as that battle with futility and death which one is going to lose, but rather as a competitive fight in which one can win.

Hence, religiously, he does not yet grasp the abysmal evil that sin is. He encounters it, as yet, essentially as a failure (so far) in achievement, an expression for a task not yet fully performed, a recognition that his ethical optimism has not yet attained its goal, but without really bringing its ultimate success into question in any genuine fear and trembling about his own salvation, reaching to the very marrow of his being as a person. If this were otherwise in a young person, it would be a sign of neurotic morbidity rather than a valid religious phenomenon. Hence a young person is all ready for active ascesis, for a sort of athletic ascetical self-discipline. In this respect, he readily accepts such tasks and demands as can be translated into concrete achievement, so long as their performance contributes to his sense of positive living, making him in some way aware of himself as an active, successful person constructing his own life for himself. For him, God is rather the absolutely unambiguous guarantee that his optimistic view of things does not have to go under to that dark side of existence which even a young person does of course see looming up here and there. God is the supreme formula which makes his youthful optimism even more direct and unqualified, rather than the object of an ultimate Yes in the midst of the experience of death.

A young person also, of course, has problems, doubts, uncertainties and disillusionments. But they are the expression of a life still on the quest for its fulfilment, not of a life which has discovered its own finitude and hence now looks only to God as fulfilment, beyond all that belongs to itself, from within the futility of life as it ebbs away. He is seeking for himself, slowly beginning to experience his own personality and take possession of it. Because he has not yet arrived at this, he is still insecure. Hence the company that he seeks is, on the one hand, that which he has chosen for himself (for it is his desire to be self-sufficient), and which on the other hand gives support to his still insecure sense of himself: his friends, "the gang," whatever changes in sociological form and structure this gang may take at different times.

If we consider all this we shall then have to say that a youthful Christian simply cannot as yet take possession of the whole of Christianity as something existentially and truly personally comprehended and realized. How is he going to be willing to grasp that a man hanging crucified on the shameful wood is the Lord who reigns from that wood? How is he going to want to understand that faith is belief in what is hidden and improbable, that hope hopes against all hope? He does not need all that as yet; though he does indeed still have to be open to it, enough of it all has to be said to him to put into his hands a sort of anticipatory scheme by which he will be able to interpret those later experiences which will initiate him into these mysteries, lest in the future he falsely interpret them into doubt and disbelief.

But primarily the specific and basic thing in youthful religion is and ought to be *God,* the mighty Lord and ultimate ground of life; God who gives life, who enlarges, who has set man a task, saying that in his glorious service we are to subdue the earth; who calls us into light, who has given each of us a great life's work, himself guaranteeing its success; Christ, close to us and loved by us, in whose army we are, whose followers we are because he is the victor, the valiant, the true, the faithful, our brother and our comrade in life; the Church, the community of those whose goal is the loftiest and whose vision of life is the most all-embracing, who are fighting for what is truly a better world and who can claim not only the distant past but the uttermost future as their own.

Youth in the Mass

This is the point from which to look at the young person's idea of the Mass and its specific ascesis. To a young person the Mass will not be so much the solemnization of the incomprehensible mystery of death, the sacramental anticipation of what must be existentially done and suffered in martyrdom and man's death. It will rather be the paschal solemnity of the mystery of Christendom, the banquet of the new and eternal covenant, the sacrament of that great thanksgiving which brings the whole creation back to God in a song of praise. It will be the celebration of the brotherly community, the meal of friendship and unity with our victorious Lord, the eternal covenant of our God's fidelity to us and our fidelity to him. The other points of view, which become existentially prominent in later life, are not negated; they are not eliminated but remain rather in the background as things known only summarily in lesson form and only indicated, in practice, in discreet outline. And these aspects of the Mass which are given prominence and are existentially lived are not by any means undogmatic aspects thought up to go with an arbitrary pedagogical method; they are part of the one complex reality of the sacrifice, and are as real, as dogmatically true and central, as the others. Hence we have a perfect right to accentuate them. This could only be denied by someone who maintained that there had never in the whole history of the Mass been any such thing as a shift of emphasis, a change in the predominant point of view. But any such assertion would be simply false.

And now of course the major difficulty begins. How is such a thing to be done in practice, now that we have thought it out and deduced it in such *a priori* fashion? We shall have to launch out a little at this point and propose (or reiterate) one or two heretical ideas, while remaining unable to make any very practical concrete suggestions.

The question is this: Is the Mass in its present form, even as influenced by the liturgical movement, such as sufficiently to encourage and facilitate its celebration by the young in general and on the lines just indicated in particular? It may well be doubted whether it is. This doubt does not involve any denial of the permanent services rendered by the liturgical movement. But can a community Mass in its usual form convey to the young that understanding of the Mass which they need? (By a community Mass in its usual form I mean a Mass in which, apart from a hymn or two, a greater or smaller proportion of the official Latin liturgical text is recited or read in the vernacular.)

Presumably we are agreed, when putting this question (since this is a point emphasized by the liturgical movement, as against older ideas), that the liturgy ought to be as far as possible self-explanatory, and not to stand in need of extraneous, time-wasting, professorial explanations. One ought so far as possible to be introduced by the liturgy into Christianity, and not introduced by Christian teaching into a liturgy which would otherwise be unintelligible. But if one starts from this principle, one may doubt whether the ordinary form of community Mass suffices for the purpose in the case of young people. For the younger ones among them, community Masses are more or less unintelligible. The texts are too lofty and internally too heterogeneous. This will also apply to a large extent to the older ones. Added to which, such Masses often become boring because the same thing is done too often (even when the nature of the thing does not call for sameness).

The official liturgical texts do not have the clarity, comprehensibility and obvious relevance to what is central in meaning and central for youth, which they ought to have if they are to convey the meaning of what is happening to these growing young people, really impressively and at once clearly and solemnly. The introit, gradual, etc., are too diversified and do not produce any clear line of thought; the Scripture readings are often too hard to understand; the central act of sacrifice between the offertory and the communion is not presented with enough clarity and impressiveness for the young by the brief Roman sobriety of the text. So long as we have to make up our minds to a liturgy which, for good reasons, does not allow any creative production of new forms for the actual liturgical action; so long as, in consequence, no account can be taken within the liturgy itself of the requirements indicated above, my opinion is in favor of a "people's liturgy" form of Mass, such as does not aspire to the highest possible degree of conformation to the official text.

This may be an heretical opinion, which seems to be somewhat contradicted by what has happened so far in the liturgical movement. But we must nevertheless ask soberly and *explicitly*, so as to clarify in theory too what has no doubt long been asked and put into practice by those pastors of youth who do not allow their vision to be clouded by idealistic prejudices: Is it possible for a form of Mass to be right for young people if it aims to approximate as closely as possible to the official liturgy? And it seems to us that the sober answer to this is No. If what I mean needs to be said in even more shocking terms, we might say: Let us come out in favor of *Mass-devotions*. Such, of course, as will strive to preserve and absorb as much as is possible of all that the liturgical movement has produced in the way of possibilities and insights. Not such, of course (like the rosary during Mass), as distract from the action of the cult, but such as provide a better initiation into what happens at Mass—better theologically, religiously, and for the needs of youth—than parallel recitation of a vernacular translation of the official texts.

The term "Mass-devotions" is obviously not important. Anyone who considers it misleading is welcome to avoid it. And if anyone can say that the forms of "people's liturgy" which we already have (which would need each to be examined in detail) already meet the demands indicated, I ask him only to test those forms once more, objectively, to see whether they already fully meet these demands or whether they could still be improved (e.g. by short introductions and responses at the beginning of Mass). He is not expected (it would not even be a good thing) to work out something completely new on these lines; it will be better to develop such forms as already exist, prudently, boldly and in co-operation.

This "people's liturgy" form of Mass for youth might then do more than is usually the case for personal devotion in communion. This is something that has very much dwindled away. And this is distressing, for young people are precisely those who would readily understand it. When we have the courage to make some sort of demands on them, when we do not simply lower the standard so as to make it attainable by all and sundry, the young are very ready to bring to communion a devotion which, on the principles laid down earlier, is, as it may and must be, thoroughly and justifiably subjective. Amongst us in Central Europe, the increase in frequent communion since Pius X has not been associated with intensified instruction on greater subjective correspondence with the sacramental action; hence, for reasons which are dogmatically easy to understand, the effects of the "eucharistic second spring" have not been as great as was hoped. As soon as the first thrill of the contrast with what had gone before had passed away, it became plain that without the personal correspondence of assiduous, interior, subjective devotion, the sacrament simply cannot have the effect proper to it.

As to what "Mass-devotions," if they were to contribute to all this, would in more detail be like, that is hard to say. In any case, the people would have to be able to manage without books. In any community, an ordinary person, not having special religious formation and not being at a special intellectual level, cannot really pray (i.e. speak in the words of his own heart directly to God) something that he has to read out of a book. No doubt the true and living word of the preacher, incorporating the Scriptures (which is something different from the mere reading of a text which remains unintelligible), would have to perform an essential function in any such liturgy. Would it not be worth while to make a few efforts in this direction, and not merely rest on the laurels of the liturgical movement? The basic achievement of the latter seems to me to consist not in the forms of popular participation in the liturgy as such which it has produced so far (since these still remain very problematical), but in having begun to establish the conviction that *the liturgy in its hitherto prevailing official form is not something unalterable,* but that it can and must be completely adapted to the pastoral needs of modern humanity.

Because the actual adaptation proceeds with understandable slowness (if only because it is being centrally directed from one point for the whole world), a "people's liturgy" will remain a pastoral necessity for a long time yet; and hence we shall have to go on doing, if in a different way, what has been done for centuries since the Middle Ages in the matter of pastoral care for the masses and for youth: celebrate Mass in a form functioning outside the official liturgy, for the sake of the people and of the young.

"Youthful" Sacrifice

However that may be, we have to see to it in some fashion (by instruction, direction, training) that the sacrifice of the Mass and young Christendom come together as the sacramental and personal aspects of one total Christianity and meet in one thing: active sacrifice. By this I mean that youthful Christianity will not be what it needs to be, what of its nature it desires to be, unless it is an active ascesis. A young person, as someone still incomplete and striving for completeness, has perhaps as yet no understanding in his personal life for that kind of sacrifice which consists in accepting the decline and death and defeat of life with its plans and possibilities. He is still too young for that.

But he is perfectly capable of understanding that form of sacrifice, self-denial and renunciation which is of necessity and as a matter of course *the obverse of all striving for greater achievement and a fuller life*. Sacrifice of this sort is not, from the Christian point of view, the whole of it; it is (if you like, and considered with reference to its immediate goal) secular ascesis, self-discipline, and that strictness which is beloved by all fighters for lofty aims. But it belongs within the Christian whole. It is a preparation for the more difficult sacrifice, the more profoundly penetrating renunciation of maturity and old age. And it is what can be understood by the young. It is always necessary. So the young must be educated for it and trained in it. And thus they acquire something which is indeed a preparation for the sacrifice of the Mass, if the Mass is to be a truly personal celebration.

Hence this active readiness for sacrifice can and should be combined with education for the Mass. A young person can very well be made to understand that the only way of being present at Christ's sacrifice with the right dispositions and properly joining in the celebration of it is by entering into the dispositions of Christ, which are here being given a mysterious presence among us in his life's sacrifice and life's work. It can be made clear to him that if what is here being celebrated is the covenant with God, ever new and ever present, by which the world is to be made more and more divine and God more and more earthly until the fullness of the kingdom of God and the consummation of his reign, then he who celebrates it must also contribute his own act, by which a piece of his own being in his own life is borne away into that fuller life in which God and the world are reconciled. One can tell him that the joyful pain felt by a brave man who is exacting in his own regard is, in customary Christian terminology, called sacrifice. And that the sacrifice of the altar is not properly celebrated without this personal sacrifice.

And inversely: if here at the Christian altar one lifts up to God his small piece of world together with the priest, so that, being changed into the body and blood of Christ, which are of the earth and belong to God, it may be a symbol that the whole of reality belongs to God and is blessed with God, then one must, here in this Mass, be resolved to go out into life and do in one's life that which has been done at the altar. One must be resolved to be a courageous fighter, a victor and conqueror; one must be able to say to oneself: "It depends on me; the 'revolution' by which the world is to be converted and return to God must begin with me; I cannot desire and expect the world to grow better, more worthy of God, more full of light, unless that which has begun cosmically and for the whole of history in the sacrifice of Christ now begins uncompromisingly in me too; the thing which I too have just been beginning in the sacred rite."

A young person needs to realize that the Mass has a glorious, joyful seriousness. Our Yes to the interior demands of grace, our Yes, not to the burden of the law, which pierces like the sting of death into the gross, froward, God-resistant inertia of the flesh only to prod it, for the first time, into real sin, but a Yes to that greater life, that wider freedom, that more embracing splendor which comes from within and is called grace and belongs to Christ, the crucified and risen; this Yes is spoken in the Mass and must be fulfilled in life. We need to consider even more closely whether it may not be possible to initiate young people into the mystery of the Mass by starting out from this grace-bearing experience which they have of being summoned to bear the pangs of a greater and happier life.

Any final, explicit, dogmatic clarification of the mysteries of faith comes, of course, from the word of the Church and the Scriptures. But this does not mean that we ought to proclaim the faith exclusively in a completely extrinsic way. If, here too, we say to the young: What you experience and undergo and endure and venerate, without knowing it, that we preach to you, then they will probably hear the message with more understanding. In our present case, this means that we should appeal to the ultimate experiences of youth, to the longing in their hearts, to the fact that they still take life seriously, that they have not yet given up, that they do not yet think of life as a dreary matter of making money, amusing oneself, and waiting, with despair in one's heart, for the end, having finally dug down to the fact that there is nothing to dig down to. We need to ask them whether they have yet experienced themselves as people with a desire to possess the whole of their lives in a greater and greater exercise of the heights of freedom; whether they feel in the depths of their being the power and the summons to make a gift of the whole of existence to that which is highest.

One would then have to tell them that of course this summons and this demand can only be fulfilled through the act of a whole long life, with its external troubles and its seeming disappointment; but that there is a holy hour, a mystical rite, in which that which otherwise only exists namelessly, so to say, in the depths of insufficiency within our hearts, rises up and takes corporeal, tangible, audible shape: in which this innermost mystery of our own hearts is united with that same act on the part of all men in all ages; in which this primal word of life is spoken in unison with the Spokesman of the whole of human history, who spoke it for us all in the dark night of his death. And that the hour in which this word, the word which sums up the whole of human existence, is thus taken up and accepted and embodied comes about in what we call the Mass.

In short, there is a path which leads from the most fundamental experience of young people to the altar, and from the altar into their lives. We can quite confidently call by the name of sacrifice that which unites the two. Only we have to make what we mean intelligible to young people, so that they will not think that "sacrifice" is an expression for that misanthropy and secret hatred of life felt by failures who are incapable of courageously enjoying life and this world and the glory of human existence.

One's "Own" Life in the Mass

There is no reason why we should not go further, and relate to the Mass the more special concrete characteristics of the life lived by individual groups of young people, and *vice versa*. Why should one not point out to the student of *language* that here in the Mass is spoken the archetypal word of the Logos;

that the Word is here in whom all things subsist, and that this Word speaks the word which is utterly effective, which contains what it says, which performs what it declares, which achieves what it proclaims, and which begins the transformation of the world into a song of praise to the incomprehensible, unutterable holiness of God?

Why should one not tell the *lawyer* that this is the solemnization of that covenant upon which all law is founded, because all law is only the manifestation and inexorability of eternal love, which in the sacrifice of the Son, the acceptance of the unrighteousness of the world, created the law of mercy? Why not tell the student of *medicine* that here we celebrate that suffering and death which are divine, and that the ultimate reason why the doctor fights against them in this world (accepting defeat by them in the end) is to make plain that out of suffering comes true happiness, and out of death, life?

Why should we not say to the man who feels that he is a creator, one who makes the world into what it ought to be, that when a piece of this world, something which has its origin in living things but is at the same time given its form by man, is transubstantiated into the body and blood of God, this confirms and exalts all man's creative powers? Why not tell him that only if he is given grace from God to make God, in the holy rite, present not only in the world but in the body of the world as his own body—that only then can he lay claim to the lesser grace not only to serve God in the world but, as a creative creature, a creaturely creator, to make this as yet unfinished world into one which, with all its deeper possibilities brought to birth, can at last praise and proclaim its one Creator as he wills to be honored and proclaimed?

When considering things in this way, one need not yield to the temptation of that art much practiced by dogmatic theologians today, seemingly theologically profound and at first sight illuminating but ultimately sterile, which consists in relating everything to everything else (St. Joseph to the sacrament of the altar, etc.). If it is true that the sacrifice of Christ is an all-embracing sacrifice, intensively and extensively, and if this is not merely "one more true thing" about it but something belonging to its immediate essence, then, while one must still not fall into that mistake which was criticized at the beginning (of conjuring the whole of Christianity directly and explicitly into the theology and practice of the Mass, so as to have everything together in a clear, one-track arrangement), yet one can say that wherever there is a striving and suffering upwards towards the overcoming of something, whether in the world or in a man, there something is taking place which is directed towards the sacrifice of the Cross and the Mass and at the same time proceeds from it. And if this happens in all such cases, then the specific kind of striving and the special kind of suffering which characterize this or that profession, this or that situation, this or that age-group, can properly, under this aspect of "sacrifice" (taking the word in a broad and positive sense), be brought into union with the sacrifice of the Mass.

In this sense every Christian, youth included, should understand his life as lived inwards towards and outwards from the altar. But this means that he has to be so guided and instructed that in the celebration of Mass he encounters the deeper content of his own life, and that from the standpoint of his life in the concrete he grasps the ceremony of the Mass in a more living way. And if this is not merely one more thing that we might perhaps think about, but a basic condition for the existential fulfilment of the Mass, if its sacramental meaning and its power are really to be given free rein, then it becomes all the clearer that we must see to it with all our resources that the concrete way in which Mass is celebrated makes this encounter between Mass and life both easy and obvious.

But it is not possible to say that mere liturgical participation in the Mass according to Schott or Bomm or in the normal form of community Mass makes this encounter between life and Mass particularly easy. In very simple, straightforward periods, when life itself was not very highly differentiated and when those (the clergy and monks) who were, without specially reflecting about it, setting the pattern for the celebration of Mass were in any case living lives with an explicitly religious character, it was no doubt possible to make do with the kind of ceremony provided by our official liturgy. It is doubtful whether this can still be said today, when the pattern of life is so much more complicated, more confusing, more interesting and at the same time monopolizes a person more thoroughly and is less explicitly religious. And we have to ask ourselves: What then is to be done, if we do not have the right or the possibility of changing the official liturgy itself? One cannot but ask oneself: Would the Mass look as it does today if, being divinely just the same as it is, it had now, in and from our age, to work out a concrete form for itself? All I mean to say by asking this obscure question is this: When we are educating people for the Mass, from life to Mass and from Mass to life, we cannot simply rely upon the official liturgy. Not even in the sense that we merely have to explain, practice and perform the liturgy and can then suppose that now everything is all right.

6

DEVELOPING EUCHARISTIC DEVOTION

Thanksgiving after Mass[1]

1. The supreme "thanksgiving" is that given in the Mass, not after the Mass. That is to say: the celebration of Mass, like any other sacramental event, involving an adult, requires personal participation; in this case, personal co-operation in Jesus' obedient, loving surrender to the Father even unto death, a co-operation which is man's thanksgiving for the salvation given to him in Christ. This thankful co-operation takes place essentially within the Mass. Expressed in ascetical terms: through the devout celebration of the sacrifice itself. Furthermore, the words and actions of the liturgy provide so many opportunities for living participation in the objective event of the *opus operatum* of the sacrifice of the Mass that our foremost task, in our instruction concerning the Mass and in our own efforts, must certainly be to make full use of these opportunities for "subjective" devotion provided within the Mass itself. Whatever happens, any thanksgiving after the thanksgiving (Eucharist) is bound to be secondary in relation to this primary task of co-operating subjectively in the objective sacramental event during its objective performance.

Hence it must be stressed again and again that a sacrament, an *opus operatum,* is not there to take the place of "subjective" devotion, nor even to make it easier, nor to facilitate some communication of grace which would, apart from the sacrament, make heavier demands on one's subjective response.[2] Rather, every objective sacramental event is meaningful and effective only in the degree to which it is realized personally and existentially. But what this applies to, first and foremost, is the celebration of the Mass itself; the "subjective" thanksgiving which takes place within and accompanies the objective thanksgiving. An objectivistically and legalistically hasty celebration of Mass, "relying" on a quasi-mechanical effect from the *opus operatum,* is inadmissible even when followed by thanksgiving.

It is undeniable that in this area of Catholic devotion there is not infrequently to be found something like a "split personality": people who, when receiving or administering the sacraments, are so full of the objective power possessed by the sacraments (and the liturgical celebration of Mass) that they think that subjective participation can comfortably be kept to the minimum required, according to moral theology, for a worthy and fruitful reception; reserving the exertions of ascetical zeal and serious personal devotion for daily life and for "spiritual exercises" separate from the sacramental life. Whereas the performance of the sacraments really needs to be the most existential of all acts; though it must of course be admitted that, taking into account the individual character of those who are not very apt in matters of cult, and also the not infrequent difficulties presented in this matter by the liturgy as it in fact exists, this ideal is not always attainable. But basically it is this unity which must be aimed at everywhere. Hence in this respect the foremost goal, when offering the Mass, is to celebrate it in such a way that it will also make effective our subjective thanksgiving for our redemption in Christ.

2. Nevertheless, "thanksgiving" after Mass is still meaningful and commendable. Given that the Mass itself has been celebrated reverently and with serious personal participation, it is, indeed, not possible to lay down thanksgiving after it as

an actual *duty:* it could not seriously be established. But we must remember that the fact that a thing cannot *in concreto* be called binding ("under pain of sin") does not automatically make it superfluous and meaningless. To assume that it does would be a typical case of legalism, i.e. of thinking based on formal obligation instead of on the nature of things; legalism such as the present generation is supposed to abominate. Such thanksgiving can indeed be meaningful, commendable, and a "self-imposed duty" for a man who is seriously striving towards a priestly way of life (and who may very well see in the concrete performance of something not obligatory in itself the very way to realize, concretely, some general attitude which *is* strictly commanded; which makes it necessary, in the concrete, *for him*). There are several indications of this, of which we shall instance a few:

(a) For many priests this thanksgiving is for practical purposes, and even in some cases unavoidably, the only form of eucharistic adoration ("visit") which they carry out.

(b) No one with a knowledge of the laws of the psychology of devotion, and of religious history, will deny that, however much we treasure the Roman liturgy, there is a certain aridity about it, a juridical austerity and a tendency to legalistic brevity, setting limits and barriers, psychologically and in terms of time, to its full subjective realization. One need only compare the Roman liturgy with that of the Eastern Church. The latter is, in a good sense, more lyrical and meditative, giving a person far more opportunity for absorption, for the free play of feeling and emotion. "Genuine subjective co-operation" certainly does not imply any special abundance of feeling, still less anything sentimental. It means the full, personal participation of a spiritual, responsible person, with his free faith, hope and love (the three theological virtues actualized), in what takes place in the Mass in terms of cult and sacrament. But participation of this sort, which precisely does *not* consist solely in a mere modicum of "good will," requires time; requires the possibility of immersing oneself patiently and meditatively, "recollecting" one's interior faculties (which are not simply subject to one's command), bringing order and equilibrium into the often highly conflicting "dispositions" at the different levels of the person, etc.; strictly requisite things which cannot be achieved very quickly.

It might indeed seem that these things should be supplied by a *preparation* for the Mass, so that the Mass itself would be, in a sense, the climax, in cult and sacrament, of a whole personal effort which, having already reached great intensity, would embody itself in the liturgical event. But given this preparation, there would surely no longer be any special psychological difficulty about thanksgiving; and preparation itself is a possibility even harder to realize, in the ordinary conditions of daily life, than thanksgiving, involving as it does that period of meditation which tends to be one of those projects that never get beyond being projects. Even given good will and interior understanding, it has to be admitted, in all honesty, that there is not enough scope and possibility within the Roman liturgy, in many cases, for genuine, subjective co-operation, which is something more than good will and more than that minimum of intention, attention and "devotion" demanded by moralists and, of course, always attainable. For this "something more," the time is too short and the formularies are too concentrated and too austere. Hence it makes thoroughly good sense to supplement what is liturgical and communal with some more private kind of "devotion" such as will counterbalance these difficulties and inhibitions in the Roman liturgy.

History, too, shows that there is a certain necessity for this: the Roman liturgy has in fact had to allow itself to be supplemented by various forms of extra-liturgical, para-liturgical and private devotion and worship, for which there is little apparent need in Eastern piety; and they would obviously not have shown such vigor and abundance if the Roman liturgy had already given scope within itself for every proper demand of "subjective" devotion. For it is just not possible to say that these forms are simply a matter of private, individual devotion, such as does of course, necessarily and everywhere, have its right and proper place alongside the community cult. The need in the Latin Church has been, on the contrary, for a great deal of worship which, while extra-liturgical and para-liturgical, is nevertheless conducted by the community.

It is significant, in this connection, that it was possible for lengthy discussion and controversy to arise over what actually is and is not liturgy in the Latin Church. It was just not possible any longer to make the simple statement that liturgy is the worship of the Christian community. We can confidently say that we do not have a liturgy within which a Latin Christian can give living expression, in adequate measure, to his own personal devotion. This is partly in the nature of things (private devotion can no more be totally equated with community worship than can the individual with a member of society); but it is also partly due to the shape and character of the liturgy as it in fact is. And this second factor would still exist even if access to the Latin liturgy had not been made difficult by the Latin language, unintelligible as it is to the people; it thus applies to the clergy as well. And because of this second factor, forms of devotion are going to exist which aim, outside the liturgy, at supplementing liturgical piety with elements which could quite well, in themselves, be provided by liturgical piety itself. (Do we not, for instance, see the "Resurrection Service" still being held in addition to the renewed liturgy of Holy Saturday?)

"Thanksgiving" is certainly one of the most meaningful and obvious among such forms of devotion. It would indeed be quite possible to imagine a liturgy which (given that it was celebrated with interior participation) eliminated the need for any such extra-liturgical thanksgiving: a liturgy, for instance, which *itself* gave scope for abundant, joyful thanks after receiving the Body of the Lord, and which looked in a more explicit and realistic way towards that daily life into which it is sending us out. But since this does not in fact exist,[3] it makes sense that thanksgiving should have become attached to the liturgy as a private extension of it. The liturgical action itself carries on into private meditative prayer.

There is also the following point: the liturgy is meant to be the consecration of life as it is in the concrete. We are not meant to have a zone of sacral existence cut off from life; life itself is meant to become divine worship, with the altar as its starting-point. But, because of its completely fixed character, textually and liturgically, the official Roman liturgy is only in a very "abstract" way the consecration of life, in the concrete, to the worship of God. Life as it is, with all its problems and needs, its exhilarations and depressions, its complexity and immensity, finds only very general and abstract expression in the official liturgy, where it is meant to be hallowed, consecrated and brought into subjection. If this sanctification of life in the concrete is indeed to radiate from the altar, then it becomes almost indispensable to create an intermediate zone between the liturgy, in its hieratic objectivity, and life in all its harsh reality, where the two can meet: a zone in which the individual strives, in personal prayer, to immerse the spirit of the heavenly sacrifice in the corporeal stuff of earthly reality. If he does take pains to bring about this encounter between the worship of God at the altar and the worship of God in life, then, with the present state and shape of the liturgy, he cannot really do without a period of thanksgiving; for this is nothing else than the action of a man, sanctified by the sacrifice of Christ, personally girding himself for the concrete act of sacrifice in his daily life.

One will be all the more ready to say this since one cannot but entertain a fairly cool scepticism in regard to the actual carrying out of the requirement of daily meditation on the part of the pastoral clergy. With conditions as they are in our part of the world, any prolonged meditation in the morning before

Mass is often, for many of them, simply not possible, even if
the will to do it is present (which it often is not, to any great
extent). Then when is the personal transposition of what the
priest has done at the altar into the reality of his own life
going to take place, if not at least during those few minutes of
"thanksgiving"? This point of departure implies, of course,
a particular kind of content for the thanksgiving, which would
need to be explained and put into practice in spiritual conferences and retreats. It is not enough to indicate in general
terms the necessity for giving thanks (with a bare reference
to the Code of Canon Law, can. 810: *gratias Deo pro tanto
beneficio agere*). For the demand that one should make a
"eucharist" precisely for having just been allowed by God to
celebrate a eucharist can hardly be made intelligible in such an
abstract formulation. It is not primarily and simply a matter of
thanksgiving, but of this personal participation in the saving
reality made present in the Mass, and its transposition into
one's own concrete life, both of which it is possible to do only
to a quite inadequate extent during the Mass itself, with the
Roman liturgy as it actually is.

In the sacrifice of the Mass, we do not, after all, merely receive the Body of the Lord as the effective sign of a grace to be
received. In this sacrifice we actively celebrate the death of the
Lord; we utter, with Christ, his eternal high-priestly thanksgiving for the creation and redemption of the world; we give
our own personal assent to the obedience of him who died for
us; we ratify, with our own faith, hope and love, that transformation of the world which was begun in Christ's death and
resurrection; in the Mass we enter, by our own free surrender,
into our Lord's own love—here celebrated and thus made present and given power over us—which wills to unite all men
more and more to the one Body of Christ; in the Mass, we renew our Lord's consent to his Cross and death as the law of
our own life; we look with expectation and confidence towards
our own future, that is to say, towards the Lord's return; we

enter, with our own nature, into the victory of Christ, into the forgiveness of sins and the coming of his Kingdom; we ratify that covenant which God has sealed with us in the blood of his Son; when we celebrate the death of the Lord, we surrender ourselves to his own weakness, his vulnerability, his subjection to death, as being the mode in which the power of God is operative in us. But if it is indeed thus alone that the sacrifice itself is rightly celebrated, if this "subjective" participation is a part of the genuine performance of the sacramental event itself, then it will be natural and obvious that the realization of these essential Christian dispositions should not just break off suddenly but show an inner tendency to carry on and sweep forward, to arrive at a more explicit confrontation with the concrete facts of daily life, which is where, first and foremost, these dispositions have to be put to the test and to prove their validity.

This gives us the point from which to understand what should be the content of this "thanksgiving": primarily, it is not so much a matter of saying a grateful "thank you" *for* something that is itself over and done with, but simply a prolongation of that inner attitude and disposition which has been (or ought to have been) actualized during the Mass. Not that any narrow boundaries are to be drawn for the content of the thanksgiving. We can safely say that anything that is genuinely devout, any movement of the heart of the person praying, his worries, his aspirations, his plans and intentions, can have their place within his thanksgiving. But we should not forget that the first place, the theologically and ascetically most important place, has to be taken by the sum of everything that belongs to the performance of the Mass itself. If participation in what happens in the Mass itself were to become fuller, deeper and more theologically articulate, then the problem of what one is actually to *do* during the thanksgiving would largely solve itself. Here again we find that the critical question posed by opposition and distaste for making a thanksgiving is whether the Mass itself is being celebrated as it needs to be.

If the need for private thanksgiving is clearer today than in former times, this is not only because of the impossibility of fulfilling this thanksgiving within the liturgy, but also because of something quite outside the liturgy: in former times a man went out of the house of God into a Christian world, understanding and control of which was based on religious principles (the important thing here being not so much whether this was achieved in the individual case, but the fact that the recognized norms were, in practice, religious, so that departure from them was generally assessed as "sin"). Today, on the other hand, the Christian is more on his own and isolated. Hence he himself has to take decisions and establish and accept norms for himself which formerly would have been proposed to the individual by society as an unquestioned common possession. Here, surely, is an important reason for the necessity of private prayer as a way of "taking one's stand" beforehand on the concrete operation of daily life.

(c) We must beware of basing our thanksgiving, on the lines of old-fashioned instruction for First Communion, on the notion that after communion Jesus Christ is "still" really present in the person who has received the Eucharist; or that because of this real presence a growth (through thanksgiving) in our dispositions can increase the effect of the sacrament *ex opere operato*. All such statements are false, or at least lack sufficient theological foundation. For the sacramental sign which increases grace is not the presence of Christ as such[4] but the eating of the Body of Christ. It ought not to be stated (because it really cannot be proved) that the real presence of Christ continues after the act of eating. For the condition for the presence of Christ is not simply some sort of physical continuity between what has been eaten and the matter that was consecrated, but *bread* as *food* in a plain human sense. But it is altogether doubtful whether bread that has been eaten can

still be regarded in a normal sense as food, i.e. as humanly eatable bread. And if it cannot, then the presence of Christ ceases
at that point, just as if, e.g., the bread were to be ground to
powder, without any chemical change, by purely mechanical
pulverization.[5] In both cases, there ceases to be any appearance of real bread in any genuine human sense; and hence the
presence of Christ also ceases.

If the impression in the popular imagination is that after
reception of the sacrament Jesus is here *"now,"* a clear distinction needs at once to be made: he is here in his spiritual
presence, in his Holy Spirit, and in a way that is deepened and
actualized by the grace of receiving the sacrament (not by any
bodily continuance). It is to this "pneumatic" presence that
thanksgiving is directed. (As children we used to pray, "Now
you are in my heart . . ."; if we had really meant by this some
abiding presence of Christ through the sacramental species, we
should, of course, have had to localize this presence in our
stomachs, not our "hearts.") It is for this pneumatic presence
that the reception, the eating (not the *having eaten*), of the
true Body of the Lord is the sign and the effective sacramental
means. Any purely somatic "presence" of Christ, if once it
ceased to be ordered to this communication of the Spirit, to
be the sign and the means for it, would become as meaningless
and as empty of blessing as the presence of Judas at Christ's
side at the Last Supper.

Even if we do suppose a continuance of the somatic presence
of Christ in the recipient after communion, it is then irrelevant as far as grace is concerned (despite the contrary opinion
of reputable theologians such as Suarez, de Lugo, etc.), because the sacramental sign is not this (supposed) presence in
the recipient, but the act of eating; it is also an unproved
theologoumenon, which, while it starts from the correct presupposition that the somatic presence of Christ lasts as long
as does the form of bread, involves the tacit and unproved assumption that bread which has been eaten is still (eatable)

bread. Nor can this assumption be proved by reference to such practical rules (rightly respectful and tutioristic in character) as are given, e.g., in the Roman Missal, *De defectibus circa Missam occurrentibus* X 14. If one does make this unproved assumption, it then becomes logically impossible to avoid drawing certain conclusions which have in fact already been drawn: that the bread should be given so resistant a character in the baking, and the wine be drunk in such quantity, as to ensure the longest possible continuance of the species.

It is also worth noting that the actual length of thanksgiving, as practiced, does not really bear any reference to the probable length of time that the species persists in the stomach. The proposition that Christ is truly eaten does not involve any presence after the eating; such a presence would have nothing to do with the eating as such. Nor can it be deduced from such propositions as those in Denzinger 578–80. For all that is stated in these propositions is that Christ is present in the act of being eaten, something that *having been eaten* brings to an end; not that Christ still remains present after having been eaten.

But this cessation of the presence of Christ in its sacramental mode, while it does mean that any increase in the *opus operatum* after the eating as such[6] is over is theologically inadmissible, does not eliminate the true theological ground for thanksgiving; nor does the direction which it has taken on the basis of this view we have rejected. The effectiveness of the Sacrament in terms of grace depends only on the dispositions which a person brings to the eating of this Bread of Life, on the existential depth and living quality of that "faith" with which Christ must be eaten, according to John 6, if a person is to enter into a truly personal communication with him and sacramental communion is to be pneumatic communion as well. But the question then arises in all seriousness: Is it possible for this disposition to be anything very much? is it possible for it to extend to the achievement of a truly pneumatic ("spiritual") communion—without which, according to the Council of Trent, mere sacramental communion would be valueless (cf. Denzinger 881)—at least in that measure and degree which is possible and desirable for the "fruitfulness" of the sacrament, if the Christian's one desire is to get out and away from the orbit of this mystery-event and back into distraction as quickly as possible? Putting it the other way round: If a Christian does develop and actualize, so far as in him lies, that interior, supreme power within him which is strictly needed as a disposition for the full significance and effectiveness of sacramental communion, then it is bound to impel him of itself to remain as long as possible (depending on the external circumstances of his life) in meditative silence and recollection within the sphere of influence of this mystery. As to the idea that the moment the liturgical event is over, this brings to an end and puts a term to the interior and exterior possibilities of remaining thus, this will hardly be maintained by anyone who has any adequate sense of the interior scope and depths of the mystery.

Thus the question of how much or how little one finds oneself inclined to prolonged silent prayer after receiving the sacrament may well amount to a very clear and applicable criterion of how much "faith" and how much personal participation one has brought to the reception of the sacrament. The impression one has that a great many of those who get out and away as soon as possible after Mass have been taking part only in a very external sense in the sacrifice itself is very apt to be justified. But one must be extremely cautious in applying this criterion to others (because one does not normally know their interior and exterior circumstances), whereas in regard to oneself it can often be a severe but extremely accurate standard of measurement. One must not commend thanksgiving in such a way as to hold back from communion people who are either prevented by external circumstances from extending their time of thanksgiving or, in all innocence, have not yet reached that degree of Christian maturity which would make such a thanksgiving intelligible to them. But an individual, on the other hand, can indeed measure his own existential seriousness in participating in the sacrifice of the Mass by his understanding of this "abiding," this contemplative resting in the pneumatic abiding of Christ within him (which lasts as long as the grace of justification).

This abiding communication with Christ, which begins with "sanctifying" grace and is increased and existentially deepened by its growth, this "abiding in him," must not be thought of as a straight factual state of affairs but is, by its whole nature, something to which the person must relate himself by faith, hope and love, something that has to be personally actualized and only thus attains fully to its own essential being. We have come to an ever-fresh contemplative realization that Christ is in us and we in him. And this personal relating of ourselves to our unity by grace with Christ is not simply a taking notice, at the human level, of a fact which in itself remains untouched by our taking notice of it, but is the perfecting of that very fact itself, since this "taking notice" is itself a self-realization of divine grace in us. But when and where should this pneumatic actualization of our abiding union by grace with Christ take place, if not when this unity by grace is given its sacramental and ecclesiastical tangibility and corporeality in our sacramental union with him, and is thus increased and deepened?

But this precisely does *not* mean that this actualization of our pneumatic communication with Christ has got to occupy precisely the same period of clock-time as our actual reception of communion in the most narrowly temporal sense of the word, or as the liturgical event of the Mass.[7] Rather, the two together can, while not being physically simultaneous, form a real unity of sacramental event, and the total pneumatic communication can be (as *one thing*) the disposition for and the effect of the sacramental reception of the Body of Christ. The mistake of supposing that actual reception of communion has to coincide in time with the personal acceptance of it is fundamentally one that could only be made by someone who thinks that there can be no union with Christ by grace except one that is identical with sacramental communion as such. But this is false, both because sacramental communion as such (the real reception of the Body and Blood of Christ) is only the sign and the means of this pneumatic communication, and also because it is perfectly possible for this pneumatic communication to take place without this tangible sacramental means. This makes it possible to see "thanksgiving" as the expression of the fact that sacramental communion and pneumatic communication with Christ are, on the one hand, not the same thing (hence thanksgiving prolonged "after" sacramental communion) but are, on the other hand, linked to each other as means and effect (hence thanksgiving in continuity with sacramental communion).

3. This provides a starting-point for saying something about the duration of this thanksgiving. Obviously this varies greatly with a person's interior and exterior circumstances.[8] Ultimately, as with all prayer, it is not a question of length of time as such but of personal intensity and depth. Nevertheless, the length of time of this meditative actualization does have an influence on its essential quality. In this respect length of time has its value. What this means for our present purpose is that thanksgiving should last as long as is necessary by a human judgment (and subject to given concrete external possibilities) in order to attain to whatever is here and now the maximum participation in the Mass in relation to one's own life. St. Ignatius Loyola says at one point in the Exercises (no. 76) that the exercitant is to linger quietly over each "point" of contemplation, without going any further, "until he be satisfied" (*hasta que me satisfaga*). He thus leaves it to

the person praying to discover by experiment and to form his own judgment on the point when, within the limits of his present possibilities, he shall have reached a certain climax and degree of sufficiency in his personal participation in this object of contemplation, thus knowing when he can go on further.

Something analogous can be said of thanksgiving, the subjective realization of sacrifice and communion. This thankful realization is not a self-subsistent, fresh spiritual event, but the subjective side of the objective sacramental event, even though it extends, in time, beyond that event. When the person performing it has "done himself justice" in regard to that sacramental event, when he has so taken possession of this thing that has been happening in sign and in truth that he is now really taking it with him into his life, then his thanksgiving is complete and it is time for him to go. If he can say that, within the limits of what is here and now possible to him, he is going out from this sacred event different from what he was when he came in to it, then he has made and completed a good thanksgiving. And his thanksgiving has not in fact been a mere private appendage to a liturgical celebration, but the completion of his personal response to the sacramental saving word of God in that liturgical celebration; a response which, ultimately understood, belongs to the celebration itself.

We might raise the further question whether, despite the personal character of thanksgiving, it might not make sense not to leave the individual entirely to himself in his thanksgiving but to have the community come to his aid. For it may perhaps often happen that thanksgiving after Mass and communion is neglected not out of any fundamental rejection of it but from distaste for the effort of prayer. Hence it might make sense to have a prayer of thanksgiving in common (not exclusively, but additionally); as is indeed already done in the postcommunion prayer, and as was for a long period the practice of the Church after Mass as well.[9]

"Visits"

1. A discussion of "visits" would need to start from everything that applies to contemplation, meditation, recollection, silence, prayer and private devotion in general. All this must here, of course, be taken for granted. But it is possible to suspect that the specific concrete problems and difficulties brought up against "visits" (i.e. prayer "before" the reserved Sacrament of the altar) are often apt to be, at bottom, problems and difficulties directed against private, prolonged, contemplative prayer in general; that the objections raised against visits as such are for the most part only a sort of ideological cover, supplied in retrospect, for a general withdrawal from the severe demands of meditation. Does one in fact know many cases of people who are really given to the practice of prolonged contemplative prayer and who also experience difficulties on the subject of visits? The question must at least be raised, with the man who is "anti-visit," of whether his objections are not in reality the protests of an activist against being called on to bring himself constantly into the presence of God, in quiet, calm, silent abandonment, and to endure the correction and purification of the silence of God.

2. It should be pointed out to the man who attacks the practice of visits as meaningless that he has no right to appeal to dubious theories drawn from the history of dogma and devotion, which are largely false interpretations of genuine facts, in order, whether theoretically or in tacit practice, to by-pass the teaching of the Council of Trent. But that teaching asserts that it is actually plain heresy to say (in theory, and hence also in practice) that Jesus Christ in the Sacrament of the Altar is not to be honored with an external cult of adoration, that he is not to be celebrated in a special feast, that eucharistic processions and "exposition" are to be rejected or that reservation of the sacrament on the altar is to be abandoned (cf. Denzinger 878, 879, 888, 889).

These dogmatic pronouncements do not, of course, clarify the inner meaning and ordering of this cult of eucharistic adoration and of the reservation of the sacrament within the totality of Christian life and liturgical action; and it is of course true, unfortunately, that in the course of the Church's history there have been periods and attitudes in Christian devotion in which (as it has been unkindly expressed) morning Mass was regarded as the consecration of a host for evening Benediction, thus bringing about in practice (and without any very strenuous efforts on the part of the official Church to counteract it) real and deplorable distortions of the perspective of enlightened Christian devotion. But in face of the definition of the Council (though reservation of the Eucharist as such is here regarded primarily as a necessity for communion of the sick) and of centuries of unanimous and spiritually fruitful practice on the part of the Church, including enlightened saints, it cannot be doubted that the honoring of the sacrament even "outside" the sacrifice, both in private and in common (in para-liturgical forms such as Benediction and Exposition) is, as such and as a whole, an embodiment of genuine Christian life and faith. (This is in no sense to defend Exposition *during* the holy Sacrifice, nor any exaggerated "visual hunger" for the sacred Host, such as leads to an indiscreet proliferation of Expositions, etc.)

What needs to be stressed is that the fact that there have been periods in which there was no actual eucharistic devotion outside the sacrifice of the Mass cannot be a valid argument against such devotion's being genuinely Christian. It would be a severe loss to Catholic devotional life if a false romanticism about the early Church led to the abandonment of what has developed in the course of the history of devotion. Christianity is history. A practice with a thousand years of history behind it has its rights, even if they are not the first thousand years. Those who exalt the early centuries into an absolute standard in matters of devotion ought to do it consistently (or

abandon it, as an absolute, altogether): which would mean
applying it to fasting, to a thoroughgoing preference and pre-
eminence for the virginal state over marriage, to the length of
the liturgy, to out-and-out monastic asceticism, and to many
other things. It is only the mind of the whole Church of all
ages that can pronounce on what is genuinely Christian, and
humble reflection on the ultimate basic structures of Christianity, which are displayed in the Church in all periods but
which do lead historically, both in theory and in practice, to
conclusions which have not always been explicit and which
yet, once given, become from then on part of the *permanent*
self-fulfilment of the Church.

It is also a very unhistorical way of thinking, since it fails
to recognize the "one-way" character of history, to suppose
that everything that appears in the Church at some particular
point in history has necessarily got to be traceable back to
some more primitive stage of the same thing. On the contrary,
in the Church as in the individual human life there are things
that come into existence and then remain. And this not only
in the sphere of theory. Now, given the clarity of these general
principles about the validity of what has come to be and is
practiced in the Church; given the emphasis, long standing,
universality and explicitness of the official Church's approval
and encouragement of Benediction, etc., in eucharistic devotion; and given that the Church refuses to abandon reservation of the Sacrament of the Altar and teaches that it is a
legitimate object of latreutic cult, then there can be no doubt
that there will always be (to a greater or lesser degree) a
private cult of the reserved sacrament. Accordingly, Pius
XII in *Mediator Dei* defends not only adoration of the Eucharist but also "devout and daily visits to the sacred tabernacle";
and the Code of Canon Law commends "*visitatio Sanctissimi
Sacramenti*" as a subject for the religious instruction of all
the faithful (can. 125 no. 2; can. 1273; cf. also can. 1265–
75: *de custodia et cultu sanctissimae Eucharistiae;* it should

be noticed that for many churches there is a *duty* to reserve the Sacrament[10]).

3. Coming now to the inner ground on which rest the meaning and content of "visits," it seems that it will not do to seek for it only and *exclusively,* as is usually done, in the real presence of Christ and the worthiness of the sacrament to be adored. For it is questionable whether this traditional foundation (correct, but somewhat restrictedly formal) is capable, if left undeveloped, of fully overcoming the resistances to the practice of "visits" which are making their appearance today. After all, the basic theological difficulty is this: True, Christ is really present in the sacrament. But what is he present *for?* So as to be there, to be with us? So as to be adored and honored as here present, as enthroned, as granting us audience? Even if we can answer "Yes" to this question—or, better, and with more dogmatic circumspection, "Yes, all this *too*"—nevertheless the primary thing is to say, with the Council of Trent, that the sacrament is instituted by Christ *ut sumatur* (Denzinger 878). The basic structure of the sacrament lies in its character as *food,* its availability for *eating.* This is the basic truth which must be our starting-point.

Because this is so, and because here in Germany, in particular, we must not forget this truth, we do not want to set up, existentially and in terms of feeling, a barrier between us and Protestant Christians (whose theology and practice of the Lord's Supper proceeds from this truth) when the question does not, objectively, give rise to this barrier. Theologically, then, it is the sentence "Take and *eat,* this is my body" that is the first and basic proposition of eucharistic theology, and not the sentence: Christ is here present. Hence Betz is right in saying[11] that the tripartite division of the tractate on this sacrament, beginning with the real presence and only then going on to deal with communion and sacrifice, is unsatisfactory and misleading "*Institutum est* ut *sumatur*" (Denzinger 878). This basic principle should, then, also be our starting-point for a theological explanation of the meaning of visits. This principle comprises within itself the real presence of Christ, for the food that is offered to us is the very Body and Blood of Christ, but it is more comprehensive, for it also says that what is given is given to us *to eat,* and we must, in our treatment of the question, do justice to this *totality* of its content.

But we come at once to an apparent difficulty. It might be said: Of course Christ is to be adored *in usu,*[12] for he is present when he is giving himself to us as the food of eternal life. But how can we be justified in going on from this basic principle to a further cult "outside" our reception of the sacrament and independent of it, distinct from this presence as food and from the adoration of the Lord which is bound up with our reception of him? The Protestant Christian, for instance, shrinks from arguing further simply on a basis of formal logic, and considers that the Scriptures give him no licence for such extensions. It is also worth noting, in this connection, that the Council of Trent makes communion of the sick the justification for reserving the Eucharist and gives no other ground for it as valid, thus correctly representing the historical situation (for it was the necessity or reasonableness of having communion outside the common sacrifice that first gave rise to reservation, not the need to have Jesus present as the "silent dweller in the tabernacle") and thus also regarding reservation as a means to the *eating* of the sacrament, which keeps the grounds for reservation well in line with the basic principle stated above (cf. Denzinger 879, 889).

If we are taking the primary biblical data as our point of departure in all this, then it must be said from the start that according to precise exegesis "Body" and "Blood" signify the whole of our Lord. What Body and Blood mean is the bodily person of Jesus, the somatically conceived Self of Jesus, one who is a living being by the bond of his life's blood and who, as the Servant of God, establishes the bond of the

New Alliance in his blood.[13] It is HE who is given. Hence it would be false to suppose that the biblical words are concerned only with his Body and Blood in some narrow modern sense of the words, so that we should have to have recourse to theological speculation and the notion of "concomitance" (Denzinger 876) in order to get from what is explicitly said by Jesus to the total reality of our Lord in the sacrament. This is not so: according to his actual explicit words, when rightly interpreted, according to their immediate sense, from the Aramaic, what he gives us is HIMSELF, so that in John 6, 57 we have simply "I" for "flesh" and "blood." He thus truly gives the whole of himself as food. Hence, adoration is here perfectly legitimate, because the food we encounter is not really something to be understood as a "thing" but is HIMSELF. To this extent, a certain treatment of the Eucharist almost as a *thing* in the early Church cannot by any means claim to be regarded as an exact and fully exhaustive interpretation of the biblical data. The medieval sense of encountering Jesus bodily as a person in the sacrament is thoroughly biblical. And hence any act that is of its nature called for by encounter with a person—better, with *this* person—is fully legitimate in biblical terms.

We now have to go a step further. According to the simple, plain word of Scripture it is what is *offered* for eating, not strictly the food that is or has been eaten, that is the Lord in his bodily reality, causing salvation and establishing the Alliance. "Christ is present as food" cannot then mean, in biblical terms, that he is present by being eaten, but that he is present *in order* to be eaten. Realism in the sacrament is the prerequisite, not the consequence, of the *usus*. On this point Lutheran Christians are at one with us Catholics as against Calvinists. Once this is grasped, then the following proposition can no longer present any insuperable difficulties: so long as this food is there as something *to be eaten,* Our Lord is there as approaching us to be received by us; and the meaningful possibility remains of encountering him as our Lord given for us and desiring to give himself to us.

Now it can safely be said that from the very earliest times Christendom has held and has freely acted on the view[14] that this food (by analogy with other foods) does not lose its character as food through having some relatively long interval elapse between the consecratory words that give it its meaning and the actual reception of it. Whenever the Eucharist is celebrated there is a certain lapse of time between consecration and reception, precisely as there was between the words of Jesus, as he handed it to them, and the apostles' act of eating. So long as the bread remains bread according to the normal human sense, i.e. so long as its suitability as food persists (this being of its very essence, since what is involved here is an essentially human concept, not a physical one), we have the presence of Christ offering himself as food, with all that this implies in an attitude of acceptance on man's side. But what this implies is not only the justification of the cult of adoration of the Eucharist but also, conversely, that adoration of Christ in the Eucharist only corresponds adequately to its object when the Lord is adored *as* offering himself to us as food, *as* the "Servant of God," bodily present in his *soma,* who has established the new and eternal alliance in his blood and wills to give himself to us, as the ultimate reality of salvation, through the eating of this bread.

If the presence of Christ is conceived of thus, then wherever he is, he is there *as* the tangible presence of our salvation, pointing back to the sacramental event of sacrifice by which this presence has been established and forward to that event in which we shall appropriate that salvation in full measure, in its sacramental tangibility as well, by reception of the Eucharist. It is not, I hope, necessary to say that the question of *which* particular sacramental particle is present in any particular case is *theologically* irrelevant: it is in any case the same Christ who is present and whom I shall be receiving; through which particular species this happens, in the concrete, is irrelevant.[15]

From this we now have the content and precise meaning of a "visit." It, too, is man's presence before the objective sacramental sign of Jesus' sacrificial death for our salvation; it is a subjective prolongation of Mass and a beginning of one's next communion. Hence everything that was said on the subject of thanksgiving applies to it, and everything that there is to say on the real meaning of preparation for communion.[16] It makes sense that they should take place before the objective sign of the cause and appropriation of salvation, the true Body and Blood of the Lord; in the presence of the Lord, present in his concrete bodiliness as sacrificial food for me in particular. Reservation of the sacrament is reservation of the Lord made present in the Mass *as such,* and of the food to be eaten *as such.* If adoration of the reserved sacrament is to avoid turning into a strange, problematical duplication of our adoration of the omnipresent God and our actualization of the pneumatic self-communication of Christ, which can be done everywhere and at all times, then it needs to proceed from *that* aspect under which this presence is actually given, and guaranteed in its significance by God in spite of God's omnipresence and in spite of our inner union with Christ[17]; under the aspect, that is, of the Lord who has offered himself upon the Cross, and who makes himself present *as such* in the Mass (and hence in the food that remains after the Mass) and offers himself *as such* to be eaten.

A person praying before the sacrament might also remember that what he has before him is the sacramental sign of the unity of the Church. In the words of the Council of Trent, this sacrament is the "*symbolum . . . eius unitatis et caritatis, qua Christianos omnes inter se coniunctos et copulatos esse (Christus) voluit*" (Denzinger 873a), the "*symbolum unius illius corporis, cuius ipse caput exsistit*" (Denzinger 875). Hence, in a visit, we also encounter him as the unity of the

194 *The Christian Commitment*

Church, and thus encounter the mystery of the Church itself, the Church in her most sacred visibility; and she, in turn, is, in her visibility, salvation made historical and tangible for us. This makes it easy to understand that the most private kind of "tabernacle devotion" is not by any means an occasion for mere religious individualism but, if rightly carried out, a realization of membership of the Church, of responsibility for her and prayer for her: an apostolate of prayer, we might also say, in a very genuine and profound sense.

4. It would be possible to arrive at the same result, for the basic meaning of "visits," approaching the matter from a different side. The starting-point here is what one might perhaps call "altar devotion." It seems to be the case, throughout man's religious history, that wherever a sacrificial cult has existed the altar has been highly venerated, even apart from the actual act of sacrifice. It is the very spot where encounter with God takes place in the cult. Hence it is a constant reminder of this, man's highest possibility. It is a permanent promise of this event. Hence it is, quite simply, the holy place. It is the place of refuge; men lay their hands upon it when taking an oath; it is permanently, even outside the sacrifice, the seat of the Godhead. All this is based on the strictly essential character of the altar, its relation to the sacrifice. But, precisely thus, it remains attached to it even outside the act of sacrifice. And this was also the case in early Christianity.[18] The altar is not merely a practical utensil for offering the Mass, used and then set aside; it is itself a permanently holy place. It is consecrated; it is held in the highest honor by the early Christians; angels stand about it; only the clergy are allowed to enter the area around the altar; people with scrupulous consciences never turn their backs on it; the unbaptized are not allowed to touch it; both clergy and laity reverence it by kissing it; oaths are taken touching it. People pray before it and, embracing it, know that they are thus embracing Christ. Hence it is also a place of refuge.

All this really means that the altar is thought of as the permanent form, in space and time, of the sacrifice, in which the Christ of God is present as our salvation (and hence as our real "altar"[19]). The practice of "visits" is in fact simply a legitimate, intensified continuation of this early Christian altar devotion. It is a legitimate culmination of it: the sacrament which remains after the sacrifice (and it is legitimate for it so to remain, because this arises from the nature of food) points much more impressively and, because of the divine institution, much more objectively to the past sacrifice and the future sacrificial meal than does the altar alone. And when the two signs are combined, the altar and the sacrificial food resting upon it, then this gives us, in the most impressive possible way, a sign in space and time, of divine institution, that Christ has sacrificed himself and now approaches us as our salvation uniting itself to us. It is before this sign that one prays. And the prayer one makes is the prayer that is the answer to this abiding, objectified Word: an ever-renewed realization of our self-surrender to the life-giving death of the Lord, acceptance of his grace, and readiness for his coming. So if anyone tries to reject "tabernacle devotion" by appealing to the fact that it did not exist in early Christian times, he must allow one to point out to him that, if he really does regard the devotional manners of the early Church as providing a standard for himself, then he must at least practice "altar devotion." But how is he going to be able to do this today, with the *sacramentum permanens* there resting on the altar, without finding his altar devotion turning into tabernacle devotion, as it has in fact done, rightly, throughout the Church?[20]

5. We can go on directly from this to grasp the connection between a "visit" and "spiritual communion"; and the theological basis of the "visit" is further strengthened by spiritual communion. We must, of course, be able to assume that it is understood what spiritual communion is.[21] If, contrary to the theology of John 6, to the whole of patristic theology, culmi-

nating in St. Augustine (but already clearly discernible in Origen), and to medieval theology up to and including the Council of Trent, spiritual communion is seen merely as a pious "as if," a pious wish to receive sacramental communion, then of course it cannot help us to see the meaning of visits. But in reality, according to the unanimous teaching of tradition, spiritual communion is in very truth personal, actualized communication, in faith and love, with the Lord in his *pneuma*. The *fructus* and *utilitas* of the sacrament are really received in it; the difference between sacramental and spiritual communion is not that between the real and the merely notional, but (setting aside a possible difference of degree, in practice, in its effect) what is lacking to spiritual communion in contrast to fruitful sacramental communion is only that which is equally present in an unworthy communion; true though it is, of course, that spiritual communion itself finds its fulfilment in the tangibility of sacramental communion and hence, even when it is "only" spiritual (which does *not* mean only mental and notional), is in its essence, and in the *votum* of the recipient, related to sacramental communion. Spiritual communion is no more a matter of "as if" than perfect contrition is a mere wish to have one's sins forgiven, or baptism of desire a mere unfulfilled wish for justification. What happens in it is rather a real communication by grace, in the holy *pneuma*, with the person of Jesus; of this, contact with the Body of Christ in the eating of sacramental communion is only the tangible sign and sacramental means, wholly ordered to serve this pneumatic communication with Christ (cf. Denzinger 881).

Hence what happens in spiritual communion is a conscious affirmation, in a personal act of faith, in love, and with reference to sacramental communion, of that real pneumatic unity with Christ which is given by the sanctifying grace of the Holy Ghost; one's acceptance of it in the personal center of oneself is renewed, and thus its ontological reality is increased and deepened. When the Council says that what happens in spiritual communion is a *"voto propositum illum caelestem panem edere"* (Denzinger 881), what this means, rightly translated, is not that what happens is a wish merely to eat the heavenly bread later on, but that in and with the wish to receive the sacrament later there is *now* a true "eating of the heavenly bread." Just as the request for forgiveness, when made in real repentance, is not merely a hopeful expectation of a forgiveness that takes place later (in the sacrament), but is truly itself the event of that forgiveness (even when it happens "merely" in the examination of conscience).

Such is the genuine doctrine of spiritual communion, which does not deserve the neglect which has widely befallen it today among the Christian people. The determining factor in this spiritual communion is not its relation to the next sacramental communion as such. We need not attach importance to the terminological question of whether we prefer to call the actualizing of our pneumatic communication with Christ-in-us "spiritual communion" *only* when it includes this explicit relation to sacramental communion, or whether this explicit relation does not have to be regarded as part of the concept of spiritual communion (*as explicit:* it is always present implicitly, if one simply cannot be spiritually united with Christ without also having the will to incarnate that union in the sacramental dimension, and so, again, to deepen it in oneself). Whichever usage we follow, it is the actualization of our union with Christ by grace, our believing and loving acceptance and "realization" (in Newman's sense of the word) of this abiding unity with Christ, that is the determining factor in spiritual communion. In the same way that what actually justifies in a *votum* for baptism or the sacrament of penance is not the *votum* as such but faith and love, so spiritual eating, in John 6, is simply loving faith; but this truly and in full reality is a receiving of Christ in his Spirit, without which "flesh" avails nothing.

But where should we be able to achieve this realization by

grace of pneumatic communication with Christ, truly present
in us by his Spirit, more readily and with more meaning than
when a man is kneeling before the Bread of Life, which is by
its whole nature simply and solely (whether we consider the
appearances or the Body of Christ which they contain) the
sign, the pledge and the promise of this pneumatic communication with the Lord? Here indeed the *"panis ille caelestis"* is
"propositus" (Denzinger 881), which is the point of reference,
in the words of the Council, of the *votum* of spiritual communion. We can then surely say that the most appropriate
context for spiritual communion is when a man is kneeling
before the altar of Christ, with the Bread of eternal Life lying
upon it. But from this the converse also follows: if a valid
tradition, with its roots in Johannine eucharistic theology,
shows that spiritual communion is a meaningful thing to do,
because it is truly an event of grace and not a pious fiction,
then we have to say the same of "visits" as well, since they
can, essentially, be nothing other than spiritual communion[22]
(even when they do not explicitly refer to sacramental communion).

From what has been said, we now see that "visits" do not
necessarily confront a person with the dilemma of either "con-
versing" with the "silent dweller in the tabernacle" and thus
having to forget that we have "Christ *in* us the hope of glory"
(though not in his physical, glorified bodily state), or else
(if one does not want and is not able to do this) to be left
wondering just why one is kneeling in front of the tabernacle
at all. As has already been said, it is not medieval but biblical
for a Christian to realize, when considering the sacrament, that
we are here given the bodily Self of the Lord, and that thus,
simply by the gracious will of God, we are given the possibility
of addressing ourselves in faith and love, in adoration and
acceptance, to that Lord bodily present to us. It has also
already been said, as part of this, that a Christian has, quite
freely, to realize the inexhaustible abundance of the reality

of the faith in a plurality of successive acts, one after the other; and that he can do this without giving way to that metaphysical scrupulosity which fears that what is, so to say, at the moment out of sight is also really out of mind and heart, merely because one is turning one's attention to something else.

All this alone is enough to show that there is nothing objectionable in a Christian's addressing himself here and now to our Lord in the sacrament, though at some other time he will find him in that Spirit which is poured out in his heart. But even apart from all this: if anyone has the charism of being penetrated through and through, right in his utmost depths, with the presence of Christ by his Spirit, then, so long as we are pilgrims who are travelling in the midst of *visible* things and must constantly *renew* our grasp of that by which we are grasped, there can be nothing but meaning and blessing in such a person's kneeling before this sacrament which is the visible surety of that to which he clings by faith: namely, that the Lord is truly in us in his Spirit (more than if he were *only* near us in the flesh). However much he may plunge into the depths of his own being, to which grace has been given, there to hear the inexpressible groanings of the voice of the Spirit and to turn himself towards Christ dwelling in Spirit in the innermost center of his being, yet it still makes sense to do this before the sacrament which is precisely the tangible assurance of *that* which we bear within us, by faith, as the light of our interior selves.

6. The point made above as number 4 does not involve the assertion that every visit to a church is to be equated with a *visitatio Sanctissimi*. For a church is not only nor even primarily a place where the Eucharist is reserved. It is first and foremost a holy space, allotted and separated from this world for God, the place in which the community assembles and thus the symbol of it. Just as the Head of the community is Christ, whose Body it is, so the church presents this Body as a building and, if the Eucharist is reserved in it, the tabernacle

is its keystone and cornerstone. But even where this is lacking, the church is still the sacred place of encounter with God, set apart by its own consecration (which, incidentally, makes no mention of the reservation of the Eucharist but only of its celebration); it is still "the church" in the sense of a symbol of the Body of Christ, "in" which a Christian can feel Christ's presence more nearly than elsewhere.

NOTES

1. Cf., on the whole of this subject, M. Viller in *Dictionnaire de Spiritualité ascétique et mystique* II, 1222–34, and the further references there given.

2. Cf. e.g. Karl Rahner, *Schriften zur Theologie* II (3rd ed. Einsiedeln, 1958), 115–41: "Personale und sakramentale Frömmigkeit."

3. When we say that in the Roman liturgy as it actually exists personal immersion in the mystery being celebrated may easily become inadequate, we must, of course, remember the following point as well: the liturgy as such must not be held responsible for the consequences of a deficient celebration of it. In the ordinary Low Mass, as it is customary today, there is in fact scarcely enough scope for a *gratiarum actio* within the celebration itself, especially for the celebrant himself, whom we are here primarily considering. But there are certainly possibilities of this sort within the Mass liturgy itself when it is celebrated in its solemn form: (a) the Communion chant, sung during the distribution of Holy Communion to a large number of the faithful, extends over a considerable time and provides an opportunity, through an appropriate text from a psalm, for both communal, objective and private, subjective devotion; (b) the pause between the *Oremus* and the beginning of the postcommunion prayer can well be filled with thanksgiving and petition following on the reception of communion, and this could then be the starting-point for a linking up with the rest of life.

4. Otherwise adoration before the tabernacle would have to have a sacramental effect too, since the exact physical distance between the host and the person praying obviously could not be the decisive factor.

5. Cf. Thomas Aquinas, *Summa theologica* III, q. 77, a. 4 c.

6. Note the "as such." What it means is that: Once, and in so far as,

the "eating" of the Sacrament (a physical and personal event) is regarded as being over (as it is by the customary theory), then we cannot speak with any theological significance of an increase of grace by intensifying one's dispositions with reference to a "still continuing" presence of the Body of Christ. But this does not answer the question whether the one act of "eating," being not a merely physiological event but a fully human act done in faith and love, must, as a whole, have reached its full completion as soon as it is over in a purely physiological sense.

7. In other sacraments, too, it is unnecessary and impossible to make a simple equation in terms of clock-time between the liturgical gesture and the personal self-commitment; the "moral whole" which they form may last longer than the physical act. The intention for a sacrament is not bound to coincide (as actual) with the sacramental rite in point of time: a person's confession may be fruitful even though he is distracted at the moment of absolution; satisfaction as part of the sacrament of penance can take place entirely "after" the rite of absolution and yet belong to the sign of the sacrament effective *ex opere operato*. The formulae of concelebration spoken by individual concelebrants do not have to be "synchronized" with that simultaneity which would be necessary in partial causes of a physical event, but can nevertheless all belong to one effective consecratory rite. It does not mean anything to ask, in relation to a sacramental formula extending over a period of time, just "when" the effect is actually produced: at the beginning of the formula, or in the middle, or not till the end; because we are dealing here with a human structure of meaning presented before God and with reference to God, and not with physical causes. Hence it is perfectly conceivable that the one single *personal* acceptance of the gift given solely in the act of eating may last—strictly as the acceptance of that gift as such—longer than the somatic process of administering the sacramental sign. We can perfectly well take account of this possibility without fearing thereby to fall in with the theory rejected above, by which a continued real presence after communion (as something temporally distinct from the reception itself) is supposed to be the basis, through some kind of second, fresh disposition (distinguishable, again, from the disposition at the time of reception) of an increase in grace *ex opere operato*. Hence we can confidently say that the personal acceptance of the sacrament (which, in an adult, is an essential element in the sacramental event if the reception of a sacrament is to be fruitful) does not need to coincide in terms of clock-time with the sacramental rite; so long as it simply has the unity

of a human act, though of a nature extended in time, and so long as its reference is to the concrete sacramental rite, this personal appropriation belongs to this concrete sacrament, even though in terms of clock-time it may extend beyond the physical period of duration of the sacramental rite both in prospect and in retrospect.

8. It must not be forgotten, in this connection, that the actual "spiritual practice" of thanksgiving, as we understand it today, cannot be traced further back in the history of devotion than the late Middle Ages. It is true that M. Viller (*Dictionnaire de Spiritualité ascétique et mystique* II, 1222–34) has managed to assemble certain medieval texts which are supposed to establish the practice. But some of them are of the late Middle Ages: some are in fact recommending a sort of holding on to the sense of adoration which one has at the moment of receiving the sacrament; and the rest are too isolated to be more than evidence of individual practice. Viller asserts that thanksgiving should normally last at least a quarter of an hour, but the reason adduced (continuance of the presence of Christ) is certainly not sound.

9. Cf. what Jungmann has to say in *Missarum Sollemnia*, Vienna, 1958, on the postcommunion (Vol. II, pp. 520 ff.) and the recessional (Vol. II, pp. 570 ff.).

10. Cf. also I. de Guibert, *Documenta Ecclesiastica christianae perfectionis studium spectantia*, Rome, 1931, nos. 542 and 543; and Pius XI's address on July 24th, 1929, to seminarians (*Enchiridion Clericorum*, Rome, 1938, no. 1467; cf. no. 351).

11. *Lexikon für Theologie und Kirche* III (2nd ed.), p. 1135.

12. Lutheran Christians, too, regard the *usus* (during which Christ is really present) as comprising the *consecratio, distributio* and *sumptio*, not only the moment of actual eating.

13. Further precisions on this point can be found in J. Betz, *Die Eucharistie in der Zeit der griechischen Väter* I, 1, Freiburg, 1955, and J. Betz, *Lexikon für Theologie und Kirche* III, 2nd ed., 1141–7.

14. Without such "reflection" based on biblical data, giving the data a concrete interpretation for purposes of concrete action, the Church can never live at all. Even when they do not seem to be cogent by formal logic, nevertheless, seeing that they necessarily had to be made (either one way or the other), and that the Church has in fact, as a whole and over long periods, arrived at them as determining her theory and, even more, her practice, it can simply be said of them that they must have had the assistance of the Spirit of the Church and that they thus carry theological weight beyond that of their formal human conclusiveness.

15. This is not to say anything against the Church's desire that, when possible, the Lord should be received in species consecrated at the same Mass.

16. Preparation is to be understood in a wide sense: realization of the relationship of the whole man to the crucified and risen Lord as him in whom alone we have God for our salvation.

17. Consider this point: there is a relationship of man to the Cross of Christ which is of grace, by which salvation is appropriated, and which is effective, even though it is not (as yet) mediated by the sacramental celebration of the Mass. Yet the Mass has meaning. For it has to be said in general that the basis of the sacraments is not that what they effect cannot be and is not effected otherwise, but that this thing that does happen *before* the sacraments and even "independently" of them constructs its own historical tangibility in space and time in the sacraments, because of the incarnational structure of the grace of Christ; and hence that it could not be received at all by someone who really, deliberately and radically shut himself against this incarnational dynamism in the grace that is offered him. Hence it is a generally applicable law that grace and the actualization of grace are possible outside the sacrament, and yet that the sacrament retains its meaning. So if it were said that "visits" are meaningless because there is always the grace of our interior union with Christ, it would also have to be said, to be consistent, that the sacraments are meaningless, because there is always grace (even without the sacraments). What should rather be said is that it is precisely that grace which already exists before the sacraments that gives the sacraments meaning, because it incarnates itself in them, and desires so to incarnate itself even where it is (in the first instance) being offered and accepted without this space-time tangibility. But precisely because the sacraments are the incarnational tangibility of grace and even, beyond this, of its acceptance, it is possible for man to gather, from this corporeal character of grace, what grace is and how he is to encounter and accept it. And hence if our spending time before the sacrament of the Body of Christ, the sacrament of the death of the Lord and of the eternal Alliance, is to correspond adequately to that in whose presence we are, the way we do it needs to be determined by the special character of this sacrament. It needs to be more than merely being granted an audience and a friendly conversation with our Lord.

18. Cf. material and references in T. Klausner, *RAC* I, 251–66; F. D. Dölger, *Die Heiligkeit des Altars, AuC* 2, 1930, 161–83; J. Braun, *Der christliche Altar,* 2 vols., Munich, 1924.

19. On the ancient theme that Christ is our altar, cf. Pauly-Wissowa I, 2, 1640–91; *DB* I, 1266–78; R. Galling, *Der Altar in den Kulturen des Alten Orients*, Berlin, 1925; M. Eliade, *Die Religionen und das Heilige*, Salzburg, 1954, 415–37.

20. A note in passing: this could the starting-point for reopening the discussion of whether the efforts being made here and there to separate the tabernacle from the altar (i.e. to render its connection with the altar, as the place of sacrifice, architectonically and optically invisible) are really so obviously right as they sometimes think themselves; or whether the official stand being made in the Church against such attempts (cf. Code of Canon Law, can. 1268§2; Pius XII, in *Acta Apostolicae Sedis* 48, 711 ff. 1956; Decree of the Sacred Congregation of Rites, AAS 49, 425 f., 1957) is not keeping in sight something essential and of permanent validity. The various equally valid aspects involved are often hard to reconcile in practice. (The decree of the Congregation of Rites referred to above does itself indicate exceptions to the practice which it calls for, of having the tabernacle *on the high altar*.) But at least it should not be forgotten, when looking for theologically and pastorally desirable ways through this problem, that altar and tabernacle do have a close, positive relation to one another.

21. On what follows, cf. R. Schlette, *Geistliche Kommunikation und Sakrament, Quaestiones disputatae* 8, Freiburg, 1959, which gives complete references on spiritual communion. Cf. also R. Schlette, *Die Lehre von der geistlichen Kommunion bei Bonaventura, Albert dem Grossen und Thomas von Aquin*, Munich, 1959.

22. At least in the sense of an explicit realization, itself grace-given, of our objective unity with Christ in the grace of his holy Spirit.

7

THE MASS AND TELEVISION[1]

If any sense is to be talked about this question, the first thing is to establish the precise point at issue. When we ask whether it is all right for the actual celebration of a holy Mass to be made the matter of a television transmission, we mean the real celebration of the Mass as a complete event; we mean that celebration as it can be seen by someone physically taking part in it, i.e. including the consecration and communion. So let it be understood from the start that the question is not whether it is permissible to bring any ecclesiastical or liturgical event to the screen, or whether it is permissible for the television camera to take in anything at all of the liturgy of the Mass. These questions do not enter into this discussion. If we are speaking about the Mass and television, the question has to be put in the form in which we have just put it: Is it right for the television camera to see, and to pass on to anyone and everyone, that which the believing Christian sees and is permitted to see when he celebrates the Church's mystery with her?

It can only confuse the issue to answer Yes with a great display of psychology, theology and apostolic zeal, and then in the end to go all embarrassed and say that it is of course bad taste and quite indecent to have the consecration on the screen, the priest just at the moment of consecration, or the actual reception of communion and things like that, because

this would be "going too far." The only right way to put the
question, theologically, is this:

Does the television camera have in principle, from the outset, the same rights as the eyes of a believing Christian?

If the answer to this is Yes, then we can no longer forbid
close-ups. If the answer is No, then this still leaves the question
open of whether there may be certain possibilities for television
in regard to certain liturgical events in the Mass; a No to this
primary question of principle still leaves numerous practical
questions of detail open, which we do not propose to answer
here. The first thing is to answer the basic question.

Preliminary

Let us say straight away that the question, thus put, must
be answered with an emphatic No. This is now to be shown.
The intention here is not to go into all the grounds on which
it might be thought possible to give a positive answer to our
question. In this regard we should merely like, by way of intro-
duction, to recall one or two points of formal logic which seem
apt to be forgotten when these grounds are brought forward.
Praise is so often given to the apostolic possibilities in televising the Mass for the benefit of unbelievers who do not go
to church. People talk about such people "looking through
the keyhole" into the church. But it is obvious that arguments
of this sort overlook something else that goes with them: that
there are things which have their psychological effect only so
long as they are accompanied by the contrastingly piquant
sense that this is different from what it used to be, that this
used not to be allowed, etc. As soon as this sense of contrast
is gone, the psychological effect is over. As soon as the televising of Mass becomes normal and taken for granted the
special psychological attraction of it, and the effectiveness of
this as apologetics, will infallibly cease. What keeps it alive is
the "keyhole" feeling with its sense of contrast, the sense of

being able to see something that one isn't really meant to see. And while we are on the "keyhole" catchword (do not those who use it to defend televising the Mass notice what a giveaway the image is? What peeping Tom wants to see is always what he has no right to see), it should draw our attention to something else as well: the fact that something can and does happen by chance, and thus *per accidens,* does not by any means give it any justification for existing in principle, "in itself," *per se.* For example, the fact that it simply does in practice happen, without the Church's intending that it should, that unbelievers are able, quite indifferently, to observe the Mass, is something that happens *per accidens.* To argue from this that it is all right to televise the Mass for everybody is to argue from what happens in practice to what is legitimate in principle, from contingence to essence, because television is something that lays itself open in principle to everybody, with equal rights for all. There is a third thing that is often overlooked when proofs of this sort are offered in justification for televising the Mass, and that is the metaphysical truth that there can in principle be quite unassimilable essential differences between things, between human procedures, etc., even though there is an apparent continuity of transition between these radically different entities.

In a Corpus Christi procession, for instance (which, incidentally, is not meant either historically or liturgically to be a showing of the *Sanctissimum* to unbelievers by way of a demonstration of faith), it does happen *de facto,* but precisely not *per se,* that everyone can see the most holy Sacrament; but this is no more a proof of the legitimacy of televising the Mass than the fact that in a particular case a person may have difficulty in distinguishing between two colors proves that "there is really no essential difference between green and blue."

Coming now to the positive proof of our negative answer, we will lay down two theses:

First Thesis

There are things that can be shown at all only if permanently subject to the control, in free consent or refusal, of the person showing them, and can rightly be seen only within this sphere by anyone else when there is a personal participation by him, a personal co-operation in the event being shown; not when there is only the naked curiosity of the mere spectator.

If, as we shall show, this proposition is sound, then it follows that there are things (events, etc.) which must not be televised. For in television the showing is of such a kind that the person or thing being shown no longer has, in principle, the possibility of excluding this or that person from this self-display. This becomes all the more valid when it is rightly emphasized (as it is, at least to a great extent) that seeing by television really is seeing, that the physical difference in the material conditions for the act of seeing does not make the seeing as such a different thing in human terms. But our proposed thesis still needs some clarification and justification. After this, it will not need still further justification in its consequences for television in general.

A man, a spiritual person as such, possesses an intimate zone into which it is permissible for another to enter only by admission of the possessor of this zone himself; and further, this admission needs to be answered by an equivalent response of participation; and it must always be possible for the possessor of this intimate zone to exclude at any time the one whom he has admitted to it. For it belongs to the essence of person and freedom that the person possesses himself (in the measure that he is a person) and hence may only be possessed in knowledge[2] and act by another (apart from his Creator) if and in so far as he himself freely opens himself.

Since the human person is of a many-levelled complexity, so that there are also impersonal, natural dimensions that belong to a man, to this extent the imperative, binding char-

acter of his personal intimacy will also have many levels. The
more personal something is (i.e. the freer it is and the more it
involves a man at the deepest level of his being), the more
it will lie within the zone of personal intimacy, and thus be
the object of a spiritual sense of modesty, prohibiting the
showing of it except as a free utterance, never passing out of
the control of the person himself, to the particular person to
whom he is addressing himself and who for his part makes
an appropriate response to it.

Whether, and how far, this safeguarding of the zone of intimacy is, simply in practice, always successful is irrelevant.
The fact that doors have keyholes does not mean that one
might just as well always leave them wide open. Purely physical and physiological matters, and in general everything that
is at the level of mere things, are remote from the central
core of the person in a quite different way from, say, an act
of personal love, the adoration of God, sin in the really theological sense, etc. Hence the utterance, the communication,
the display of the one set of realities may well be addressed
to all, whereas the revealing of the others is essentially something reserved and limited; the very nature of man, not only
in the religious sphere, demands something in the way of a
disciplina arcani. And what comes under it consists not merely
of the personal events strictly as such (these not generally
needing, indeed, to be protected against the prying of any
curious outsider), but also of the bodily realization of them
in the dimension of bodily humanity, in as much as the embodiment of these personal acts of the spiritual person is, in
the concrete, constitutive of the acts themselves, being indispensable to them. Thus it is generally allowed that, for
instance, the confession of sins, certain expressions of personal
love, and certain religious acts are of their nature not such
as to be automatically on view to everyone. The fact that ways
of protecting this zone of personal intimacy, and the precise
boundaries of it, have shown wide variations in the course of

human history does not contradict what we have been saying but confirms it.[3]

Second Thesis

But if there do exist events which may be shown only if permanently subject to the free control of the person showing them and be seen only by someone who co-operates with them in an appropriate response, then holy Mass is in the highest degree such an event. It is, if ever anything was, a matter for that metaphysical sense of modesty which protects the personal center, and its object, the sacred, against the clutchings of mere curiosity.

This holds good, in the first place, if we consider this event from the point of view of those celebrating the Mass. It is permissible for them to perform the objective sacramental mystery of the Mass only if they bring to it a quite definite personal participation in faith and love. A merely objective setting-up of the external cult-action without personal co-operation in it would be a sin and sacrilege. The Mass is thus necessarily and essentially the embodiment of the most intimate religious acts of which any man is capable. But these acts, as was said above, are subject to the dictates of metaphysical modesty. It would be shameless in the highest degree to perform them in the sight of any and everyone's indifferent curiosity. As to whether everyone in fact feels this to be so, this is quite irrelevant to the answering of an essential question like this; not feeling it may easily be due to the fact that custom, etc., has greatly reduced this sense of modesty. Acts of this sort belong either in that inner chamber where only our Father in heaven sees us, or in the sacred community of those who are all filled with same Spirit of God.

But the same conclusion is reached by considering the objective event of the celebration of the Mass itself. In the first place, it should surely strike doubt into the defenders of the

televised Mass when they consider that their idea leads straight
to a complete denial in principle of any *disciplina arcani* what-
soever; for having the Mass on television can only mean admitting absolutely anyone and everyone to the innermost
mystery of religion. Yet up till now there has always been, in
every religion, some form of this "discipline of the secret"; in
paganism, too. The temple (and what goes on in it) is, as its
very etymology indicates, a sacred place set apart, and hence
not in every respect open to everybody. There was also a discipline of the secret in Christianity. Though it is true that the
rigorous *disciplina arcani,* probably modelled, from the third
century onwards, on the *disciplina arcani* of the mystery cults,
disappeared again after a few centuries, nevertheless it is also
true that even before this Christianity had the feeling that the
central core of its most sacred cult could not be open to everyone in general.

This can be seen already in the Acts of the Apostles (9, 5;
14, 2.) The feeling still remained in the Middle Ages. While
the various kinds of excommunication, suspension and inter-
dict are primarily to be regarded as ecclesiastical punishments
for faults, yet underlying them is the conviction that the
Church's cult cannot simply automatically be open to everyone. It would be a mistake arbitrarily to assume that unworthi-
ness in this sense to take part in the central cult of the Church
must always necessarily depend on a personal fault in the
person who is to be excluded. In canon 2259 §2 of the Code of
Canon Law[4] we have an ancient relic of the *disciplina arcani*
as laid down by law. The fact that, in accordance with the
times, the legal form of this discipline has shrunk to something
very small does not by any means prove that these mere legal
requirements are all that constitute the *disciplina arcani* as
such. The disappearance of the grounds for any positive, legal
prescription (or the impossibility of laying down any such
rule for a great many cases) does not at all rule out every form

of the *disciplina arcani* as arising from the nature of things—
from the natural law.

When the theologians of William of Auxerre raise the question, in the Middle Ages, of whether sinners are permitted to
witness the Eucharist, this is a real question for them, and it
shows that they still had an understanding of a religious sense
of modesty and of the *disciplina arcani*. Even though they
answer the question affirmatively, this does not tell against our
theory. For a sinner is a member of the Church, and is such
precisely within the dimension of the Church's visible cult, so
that he does not need to be excluded from all participation in
that cult which would involve seeing the Eucharist. That this
does not justify laying the Eucharist open to every kind of
profane observation is explicitly shown by St. Thomas
Aquinas, when he remarks that an unbaptized person is not
permitted to see the Eucharist.[5] Thus the Middle Ages still
shared the feeling of the early Church as witnessed to by St.
Ambrose, when he tells how his brother Satyrus did not dare,
as an unbaptized person, to behold the Eucharist.[6] We find Hus
still agreeing with the teaching of St. Thomas on this.[7] Even at
Trent the question was raised of whether and how far it would
be desirable and possible to exclude heretics from holy Mass.
It was only the difficulty then existing of distinguishing in the
concrete between heretics and Catholics that led to the abandonment of such a regulation.

If, then, there is in religion and in Christianity anything at
all that is so sacred as to belong within a space set apart from
the profane world, namely the temple formed by the communion of saints, then that thing is the most central cult-action
of the Church, the mystery of holy Mass. Not only because it
is the bodily performance of the most personal of all acts on
the part of the faithful, such as naturally belongs within the
sphere of personal modesty; but also because the Mass is in
itself the bodily manifestation of the grace of God, the presence of the Son of God and his Cross: the Holy Thing which,

at the very least, demands not to be proffered to just everybody by the person at whose disposal it is placed.

Let it not be objected that, in the incarnation, Love-made-flesh did indeed choose to reduce himself to the absolute profanity of this world and put himself within the reach of everyone. For in the first place it is not for us to dispose as we think fit of this Love who thus exposes himself to the world, or to suppose that we are automatically justified in doing what he himself did in descending once for all to the profane level in his death. Secondly, our Lord's way of acting after his once-for-all victory on the Cross (in which it is precisely the holy as holy that remains victorious over its absolute profanation by the world) shows that from now on he does not choose simply to remain exposed to the profanity of the world and to appear as such; for after his resurrection he no longer appears to the religious rank-and-file but only to witnesses preordained by God (Acts 10, 41). Hence the sacramental activity of the Church must show forth both sides: the tangibility of the sacraments shows forth Christ's presence with us in the world, while the separation of the sacramental event from the world shows forth the fact that Christ is not of this world, that he has saved his own out of this evil world, that he does not pray for the world (John 17, 9), and that his own cannot share the table of the Lord with those who are without.

Precisely because what is involved here is the dimension of cult and sacrament, this separation between those who are admitted to Mass and those who are excluded from participation in it does not imply any judgment on the relationship of either category to God in the depths of their consciences. But assuming that those who are outside are in the grace of God precisely does not mean that they therefore have equal rights in the dimension of the cult. Otherwise it would mean that we should have to be able to administer the Eucharist to all non-Catholic Christians.

The Microphone and the Television Camera

It cannot be objected that, if the microphone can be brought into the liturgy of the Mass, the same right must be accorded to the television camera. For in the first place, it certainly is possible to ask whether the microphone does in fact have the same rights as the powers of hearing of the faithful. This is by no means unquestionably the case. In the Latin liturgy this problem is not very acute because the central prayers of the Canon of the Mass are not audible even to the faithful who are present, and hence are inaccessible to the microphone. But beyond this, it must be noted that to speak about an event and to admit someone to an event are not the same thing. Imparting something about an event and personally performing that event are very differently related, in degree of proximity, to the personal spiritual center of the one who is doing the imparting or performing; hence quite different norms apply in the matter of admitting others to such a communication as opposed to the event itself. A religious sound-broadcast is fundamentally no more than a further technical means of imparting objectified ideas, as is done in a book. In face of the existence of Holy Scripture it is not possible to doubt that the existence of a book with a religious content, indeed the word of God itself, is humanly and morally justified, however little one ought to take this fact for granted as something obvious from the start, and however much one may wonder whether it would be possible at all in a world that was only the world of sin and of the Cross. However that may be, the word thus written and transmitted is a word, and its content is separable from the personal fulfilment of that content in faith and love. It is, besides this (when it is indeed being legitimately addressed to the whole world), an invitation to faith, and hence can be addressed to each and every person, whether in a book or in a broadcast.

But this is by no means to say that it is all right to broadcast everything whatever that is acoustically accessible. When what is audible is indissolubly bound up with the kind of personal act which is subject to the law of personal modesty, it must not be allowed to be heard by everybody in general. It was possible for the Curé of Ars to weep in the pulpit because, and in so far as, the people before him were religiously at one with him, even though there might *per accidens* be someone else there. But a person speaking into a microphone in a studio is *per se* addressing himself to all his listeners, and for him to exhort them with tears would be a spiritual shamelessness. This should enable us to characterize more precisely the style and content of a religious broadcast. One cannot send through a microphone everything that can be said within the sacred assembly of those who are filled with the one Spirit of God. Thinking this over will make it clear that religious broadcasting and religious television are not simply subject to the same law, and that, where they are the same, indiscriminate transmission to everybody is equally forbidden to both.

Conclusion

If Mass is one of those events which must not be displayed to any and everyone; if, on the other hand, televising an actual Mass involves an essential and not merely incidental showing of the Mass to everyone, then the following conclusion can be drawn: such a television transmission offends against the commandment that our most intimate personal acts, and that which is holy, are to be made accessible to another only in the measure to which he is able and willing to participate in them with a personal response; while he who is showing these acts and this holy thing must retain throughout free control over the whole showing of them.

If it would be in the real sense of the word a spiritual indecency for a Christian during Mass to study, in an attitude of religious indifference and mere curiosity, the faces of those who are reverently worshipping there, so is it even more a contradiction of the law of personal modesty and of reverence for the sacred to have a film camera "observing" the priest at the consecration, adoring Christians shown in close-up, priests and worshippers selected for the "photogenic" quality of their faces, the sanctuary cluttered up with apparatus. What is the point of all this nuisance, which is already with us or threatening us? The conversion of unbelievers? Those of them who are already seriously seeking and inquiring are not going to find the road to church too long. Moreover, even the most primitive understanding of the liturgy now calls for some preliminary knowledge. Without it, the effect of the liturgy is anything but "attractive." Not long ago in Hamburg the weekly news program showed the liturgy of the creation of the cardinals; it was greeted by "intelligent" viewers with gales of laughter. It simply cannot be otherwise. Something has to be known in advance of the liturgy, i.e. of its content, or else it cannot, as it now *de facto* is, have any attractive effect. But anyone who possesses this prerequisite will be led, by his own interest, to the church itself. The rest will sit in front of their television sets in the same state as we would be if such a program confronted us, against our will and to the detriment of decency, with the religious customs and ceremonies of Tibetan monks.

Is the idea to bring great and unusual ecclesiastical events to the faithful, who cannot directly take part in them? Television can do this without the television camera's being allowed access to what is only permitted to the adoring gaze of the faithful.

Or is it to console the sick by the televising of Mass? Logically, one should begin by observing that television has to be proved legitimate first before any use can be made of this particular advantage. To try to deduce such a legitimacy from it is absurd. One might as well prove that beer could, in case of necessity, be used for baptism. Finally, the same applies to the sick as has just been said about televising great and unusual ecclesiastical events.

There is a final point that should not be forgotten. Straining to be as modern as possible soon shows itself up as completely out-of-date. Once television becomes part of the ordinary person's ordinary furniture, once he is accustomed to looking at anything and everything between heaven and earth that strikes the eye of an indiscriminately curious camera, then it is going to become an extraordinarily exciting thing, for the ordinary man of the twenty-first century, that there do still exist things which cannot be looked at sitting in an armchair and nibbling a sandwich. It is going to be an indescribable blessing to this man of the coming centuries, if there is still a place—the church, in fact—where he can still retain his full natural human size; where he does not have to look at himself and his body as something archaic, a mere leftover in a world of machines with which he surrounds himself and almost tries to replace himself; where he still has a place that will continue always to heal him of his own insignificance in the midst of technology—which is indeed his task and his destiny, but can avoid being his ruin only in the degree to which he manages to retain in his life a space too, as of old, for what is merely human, what is on a small scale, what is directly bodily. There are many matters in which the Church could well be more modern than she is. But the time is beginning already in which having the courage to be old and human is going to be the most modern thing of all. The Church, who thinks in centuries and is not easy to outlive, does not need to use a television camera so as to let an unbelieving world stare dully at the performance of her loftiest mystery until such time as this sensation, too, shall have become just another bore.

NOTES

1. From *Apparatur und Glaube, Überlegungen zur Fernübertragung der heiligen Messe*, with contributions from Romano Guardini ("Photographie und Glaubenszweifel"), Clemens Münster ("Mysterium und

Apparat"), Fritz Leist ("Ferne und Nähe"), Heinrich Kahlefeld ("Das Heilige den Heiligen"). Published by Werkbund-Verlag, Würzburg, n.d.

2. Knowledge too is a taking possession of what is known, a relation to the thing in itself!

3. This is the place for a further note. It is possible to show more in a play than in reality, because, whatever illusions may be fostered by actors and audience, a play is and cannot but be performed in such a way that it remains, consciously, a play; the same applies to pictorial representation. Because what the play and the picture show is not shown as real the same axioms do not automatically apply to them as we have been developing for the showing and viewing of a real event. Hence it cannot be said that whatever it is permissible to represent in a picture or play can also be televised. For what television aims at is precisely seeing reality as such.

4. This canon deals with the conditions under which an excommunicated person is to be excluded from presence at Mass, failing which the celebration of the Mass is to be stopped.

5. III q. 80 a. 4 ad 4; IV Sent. dist. 9 a. 3 q. 6.

6. De excessu fratr. Sat. I, 43; and cf. St. Augustine, In Ioan. tract. 76 n. 3.

7. IV Sent. dist. 9 n. 3. On the whole historical side of the question, cf., e.g., O. Perler, "Arkandisziplin" in the *Reallexikon für Antike und Christentum* I, 667–76, and the references there given; E. Dumoutet, *Le désir de voir l'hostie*, Paris, 1926; P. Browe, *Die Verehrung der Eucharistie im Mittelalter*, Munich 1933; J. A. Jungmann, *Missarum Sollemnia* I, Vienna, 1946, pp. 150 ff. (Eng. trans. *The Mass of the Roman Rite, Its Origins and Development*, New York, Benziger, 1961); A. L. Mayer, *Die heilbringende Schau in Sitte und Kult*, in *Heilige Überlieferung* (Festgabe I. Herwegen), Münster, 1938, pp. 234–62, esp. 255 ff.